*"Mountain madness!
How easy to come by and
how hard to lose!"*

Helen Hamilton, 1922.

Publication Information

ISBN 1-55153-913-6

Cataloguing in Publication Data
Cavell, Edward, 1948-
Rocky Mountain madness

First ed. has title: A celebration of the mountain dwellers and pilgrms...who have been affected by Rocky Mountain madness...campfire tales, newspaper accounts, reminiscences, and letters.
Includes bibliographic references.
ISBN 1-55153-913-6

1. Rocky Mountains, Canadian (B.C. and ALta.)--History--Anecdotes.* 2. Mountaineering--Rocky Mountains, Canadian (B.C. and Alta.)-- Anecdotes. I Whyte, Jon, 1941-1992. II Title
FC219.C38 2001 971 C2001-910732-3
F1090.C38 2001

We acknowledge the financial support of the Government of Canada through the Book Publishing Industry Development Program (BPIDP) for our publishing activities.

Printed in Canada by Friesen Printers
10 9 8 7 6 5 4 3
Altitude GreenTree Program
Altitude Publishing will plant twice as many trees as were used in the manufacturing of this product.

Front Cover: Elsie Brooks and a bear, circa 1920; *Byron Harmon*
Back Cover: Swimmer at Berg Lake, Mount Robson, 1924; *W.S. Park.*
Frontispiece: Climbers on the summit of Mt. Resplendent, Alpine Club of Canada Camp, 1913; *Byron Harmon.*
Opposite: On the brink of the Columbia Icefield, circa 1925; *Caroline Hinman.*

Design: Stephen Hutchings

Altitude Publishing Canada Ltd.
1500 Railway Avenue
Canmore, Alberta T1W 1P6
1-800-957-6888 • Fax 1-800 957-1477 • www.altitudepublishing.com

A Celebration

of the mountain dwellers and pilgrims, the guides, packers,
wranglers and cooks, jinglers, tourists,
Indians, climbers, painters, Mounties,
writers, jitney drivers, photographers, poets, bears,
shopkeepers, hunters and sportsmen, skiers,
ne'er-do-wells, romantic fools and sweethearts
who have been affected by

Rocky Mountain Madness

who have lived in or have visited the Rockies and Selkirks of Canada
and who are herein held up to a light of their own making
for our delectation and observation

An Historical Miscellany

including accounts of occasional accomplishment
accomplished adventure
adventurous rambling
and rambling discourse
campfire tales, newspaper accounts, reminiscences, and letters

A BitterSweet Romance

served by

Edward Cavell

who chose the photographs and

Jon Whyte

who selected the words

and presented to the public by

Altitude Publishing

The Canadian Rockies and Vancouver, Canada

MADNESS REVISITED

Revisiting this book almost twenty years later has been a joy as well as a nostalgic indulgence, much like meeting up with a bunch of long absent friends and putting another log on the fire...as it were. In this new edition we have tried to be as true to the original as possible but the new format has required some compromises. A few of the longer pieces were shortened and several texts and photographs deleted. We couldn't resist adding a hand-full of new, classic photographs.

"A fair kodakerist," Miss Job, Alpine Club of Canada Annual Camp, Lake O'Hara 1909; *F.W. Freeborn*

When *Rocky Mountain Madness* was first published in 1982 it was dedicated to Catherine Robb Whyte, an American artist and socialite, who married Banff-born artist Peter Whyte and was captured body and soul by these mountains. She spent the balance of her life celebrating the intense beauty and rich history of the Canadian Rockies, eventually establishing the Whyte Museum of the Canadian Rockies whose collections Jon (her nephew) and I mined so assiduously. Jon in turn dedicated his life to this larger-than-life place of his birth. A certified eccentric, passionate poet, stalwart environmentalist, muse and friend, Jon inspired, coaxed and badgered a new generation of artists, writers, film makers and photographers into celebrating and recording the phenomena of mountain life. His death in 1992 was a true loss.

Jon and I made the rough preliminary selection of words and images from the extensive resources of Banff's Whyte Museum. To form the final product we were joined by our friends and publishers, Carole Harmon and Stephen Hutchings, founders of Altitude Publishing. In a series of lively—though often intense—meetings, each photograph or excerpt was argued for, traded against, used as a bribe and staunchly defended. The resulting book is as quirky as the four of us who, like the subjects of the book itself, have been sorely effected by this Rocky Mountain madness.

Edward Cavell, May 2001

Banff Avenue, 1887. Some say the cow belonged to George Steward, first superintendent of the National Park; others say since the Brewsters owned the dairy, it is likely a Brewster cow. Nor is the name of the cow's attendant known.

"IT WAS A REAL PLACE THEN"

Just a century ago the Rockies began to get busy. In the century before, occasional fur traders, Indians, map makers, missionaries, and explorers had reached the intersecting valleys of the ranges. But not until the railway pierced the wilderness did settlement, exploitation, and tourism begin in earnest. In 1883 the CPR main line reached what would become Banff and Laggan, and another twenty-five years would pass before the rails reached Jasper and the Yellowhead Pass.

It was the heyday of Victorian ambition. The sentinel peaks, hitherto a silent barrier, suddenly became a playground in which climbers, hunters, painters, photographers, and writers scrambled in a madcap game of "King of the Castle" played upon summits of spectacular beauty. The urge to conquer and name, describe and define, and to understand the world is what summoned so many brightly vigorous and ambitious people to the Rockies and the Selkirks. A complex maze of confusing routes, secret—some would say sacred—valleys, dazzling glaciers, daunting peaks, and the mystery of the sublime were challenges both to the imagination and the more resolute characteristics. We can be grateful now for the sophistication that accompanied the Victorian madness for mountains, a sophistication which far outstrips our own. On their way through untracked valleys, our precursors paused to draw maps, take fine photographs, scratch up the provender to stay alive, analyze the rocks and geological structures about them, execute fine paintings, all the while plunging into the unknown but writing wonderful accounts of their adventures in exhilaration and persistent wonder.

If in their excess—and who among us would dare to suggest they went too far?—they sometimes appear silly and wear motley and play the clown, then so be it. Few of us could undertake journeys and adventures of equivalent trial.

Banff, surely one of the very few settlements in the world to develop and exist as a resort from its start, also took on the exaggerated swagger. For thirty or more years it was the most sophisticated town of western Canada (the competition was not heavy), a watering hole for the elite of eastern Canada, the United States, and Europe. But it was also a rustic—albeit bucolically charming—outpost of the Empire, and a crowd of zanies peopled its streets in the guise of packers, outfitters, cowboys, cooks, guides, merchants, and entrepreneurs. "What was Banff like when you first arrived?" someone asked Jimmy Simpson, guide, trapper, hunter, resort owner. He replied, "Well, we used to play poker in the police barracks, and we used to play polo where the Mount Royal is; we didn't have a decent Main Street until R.B. Bennett lost one of his rubbers in the mud and said, 'I'll have this damn street paved.' What was Banff like? It was a real place then."

But isolation for nine months of the year and the lack of an industrial base other than tourism distinguished the village from western Canada's other settlements and cities. Melancholia—black humour—erupted in crustiness, the shell of humour we devise to protect ourselves, a lesser form of madness. Jimmy Simpson, for example, suggesting that tourists are just like Columbus: "When they leave home, they don't know where they're going; when they get there, they don't know where they are; and when they get back home, they don't know where they've been." How would you react if your turf was invaded every year by so many people you had difficulty locating a crony on the street?

Rocky Mountain Madness we hope evokes both senses of "madness": the mania for mountains; beauty and challenge, and the capricious antics that mountains can summon. The book is not a set of chronicles, nor have we adhered strictly to the sombre measures of time. There is a frisson in the image of the parade which suggested a variation in the sequence.

Crossing White Rabbit Pass, 1924; *Byron Harmon.*

The texts have frequently been shortened, and the photographs are infrequently placed in a one-to-one relationship with the texts. Since we were not preparing a scholarly book, we have not indicated our deletions, but we provide the sources for those who wish to be more deeply engaged. We have let stand spellings, names, and punctuation of the original publications, cleaning up only the obvious typographic errors. The cutlines for the photographs usually indicate such information as is available to the best of our knowledge.

Enough of business. Even now the distant whistle of the train is heard, and tumbling, energetic players are waiting in the wings. Let avalanches be the drums; let the wind in treetops be the flutes. Let the stage be set. Let the parade begin.

Jon Whyte and Edward Cavell, spring 1982

Ebenezer William "Bill" Peyto at his cabin near Simpson Pass, August 1913; *A. Knechtel*

West to the Mountains

Jim Simpson letter to Dr. J. Monroe Thorington AAJ 1976

At the time when the railroad was finished as far as Calgary, a rich English lord arrived to make an exploring journey in the mountains. He engaged two packers, Tom Wilson and Fred Stephens, and eight horses. On the very same day they made a long trip to Kananaskis, stopping there for the night. The first packer got supper ready, while Stephens fixed up the sleeping tent for the lord. When the meal was ready Fred called the lord to eat: "Supper is ready, don't wait, it gets cold." The lord came out of the tent and saw, to his great astonishment, that the two had already started in. So he shouted in his London dialect; "By jove, don't you know, I am not accustomed to eating with my servants." "Goddam," said Fred, "If you are not, then just wait!"

Walter D. Wilcox, The Rockies of Canada, 1909

Quick and cool in time of real danger, Bill Peyto has too much anxiety about trouble ahead, and worries himself terribly about imaginary evils. He sleeps with a loaded rifle and a hunting-knife by his side. "Bill," said I,

Tom Wilson, Banff Avenue, circa 1905; *Byron Harmon*

one night, upon noticing a row of formidable instruments of death near me, "why in the mischief do you have all of those shooting irons and things here?" "I tell you," said he, with an anxious look, "I believe this country is full of grizzlies; I heard a terrible noise in the woods this afternoon, and besides that, they say the Kootenay Indians have risen. They may come into the valley any night."

MEMORIES OF GOLDEN DAYS

Tom Wilson — CAJ, 1922

It had been raining all spring and summer, the worst we ever had in the Mountains. I had come down from the head of Quartz Creek and recorded my claims (Judge Vowell and Redgrave had opened the office at Golden while I was out in the Hills) and then went to end of track for more supplies. I came back to Golden—still raining—and thought I would get a leave of absence from my claims on Quartz Creek, until the end of track reached the Beavermouth. The Sheriff said I did not need it for a quartz claim, but I insisted and asked him down to my tent on the banks of the Kicking Horse River—still raining. We put a log on the fire and talked some more and went back to the office, and he wrote it out for me.

A lot of the boys had come in from the Hills to record claims and get supplies and it was getting late and still raining, and the 21st August was my birthday—so we went back down to the tent and put another log on the fire. Shan and Jock McKay joined us, and we put on another log; then the Sheriff told us about his favourite saddle horse that had learned to retrieve for him, when he shot any ducks or geese on the river or slough the horse would go in and bring them out to him—same with fool hens or grouse on the trail. Shan looked sorry for a while, and then said he believed him. We put on another log, and Shan told

Heavy snow near Poboktan Creek, 1924; *Byron Harmon*

the Sheriff about a marten that he had trained—up on the Middle Forks—to lead other marten to his traps—said he got the idea from their having a trained steer at the Chicago stock yards to lead the wild ones into the slaughter house. The Sheriff said he believed him—about the trained steer. Just then Archie McMurdo and Dutch Charlie joined the fire, and we put on another log. Archie said he was having a lot of work picking the rock out of the gold on his claim up in the Caribou Basin. Dutch Charlie said he was going to buy the C.P.R. and finish building it himself—said Jim Ross was breaking all the contractors that wasn't in the ring, and robbing those that was.

Then one-eyed Jim Kane and Tom Wright joined the fire, and we put on another log—still raining. Jim Kane said he was only going to bring in a small sack of gold at a time from his claim on Canyon Creek, didn't want to hurt the Market. Tom Wright said he was going to buy some good lumber as soon as the end of track got to Golden and build him a big houseboat—said it was just this kind of weather that gave old Noah the tip to build his. We put another log on as Ben Pugh and Tom

Opposite: Elliott Barnes giving a photography demonstration on the Kootenay Plains, circa 1908; *Mary T.S. Shäffer*

Haggerity joined in. Ben said he had not struck anything but indications of a dam hard winter. Fred Aylmer and Baptiste Mougeau came over from the store, and we put on a branch or two. Then Frank Armstrong and Arthur Dick and several others came to see if it had stopped raining. At daylight most of the crowd had retired, still raining. Archie had curled up under the little spruce tree and wanted to bet anybody that the only good dry place in the Valley to strike a match on was his tongue. I packed up and hit the trail for the end of track.

Good old days on the trail and evenings around the Campfire, and when the coffee pot upset just as it was beginning to boil and the sugar and salt got wet, and sometimes the beans went sour and the bacon musty and the wind blew the smoke in your eyes, and the ashes and sparks on your blankets, the butt of the biggest bough hit the small of your back, and the mosquitoes almost crowded you out of the tent, and you heard the horse bell getting fainter and fainter, and you knew damn well they would be five miles away in the morning—but just the same, O Lord, how I wish I could live them all over again.

The Surveyors Arrived in 1881 and 1882

Charles Aeneas Shaw, Tales of a Pioneer Surveyor

Early in March 1883 James Ross asked me to return west as soon as possible, to prepare for the season's work. Ross discussed a general outline of plans for the season's work, then said, "I have a profile here I'd like you to look over. It's a nightmare to me and I'm afraid it will hold us back a year."

He unrolled about sixty miles of exceedingly heavy, difficult work, with a mud tunnel—that abomination to en-

CPR woodburners, 1887-88; *Boorne and May.*

Three Sisters, August, 1903; *Beatrice Longstaff Lance.*

gineers—over half a mile long. When I asked him where this line was, he said, "It's the final location of Rogers' line from Calgary to the gap."

Examining the plan, I found that the line followed the north side of the Bow River all the way. I at once said, "I can get a far better line than that."

At this a man who was working on a plan became wrathy and, springing up, said, "That's the best line that can be got through that country. Who in hell are you, any-

Banff station, designed in a quick sketch Van Horne drew on the back of an envelope; September, 1900.

way?" The speaker was Major Rogers, whom I had not met before.

I told Ross, "I will take my party out and locate the line from Calgary to the gap. If I don't save at least half a million dollars over the estimated cost of construction of this line, I won't ask any pay for my season's work."

> *"The most extraordinary blunder I have ever known..."*

This made Rogers so angry that Ross thought there was going to be a scrap, so he winked at me not to say anything more.

In running the line from Calgary to Morley the work was made very unpleasant by the dead cattle; every ravine we came to was piled full of them. They had drifted in during the storms and, piling on top of each other, had perished. There were also many dead animals in the river. I remember one night at supper, after moving camp, I took a mouthful of tea, but found it so nauseous I had to spit it out. I asked the cook what was the matter with it; he could not explain the trouble as the water was from the Bow River. Next morning we found a bloated dead cow in an eddy a few feet above where the cook got the water.

After completing the line to the gap, and while awaiting further in-

Party at Sawback section house on the CPR line just west of Banff, including Lizzie and Dave White (seated at left) and Bill Peyto standing on the front of the right-hand speeder, circa 1897.

structions, I continued the location west, and had some miles completed when Ross, the Chief Engineer, arrived. I asked him if I had made good on my undertaking to save half a million dollars on the line from Calgary to the gap.

He said, "The estimated cost of constructing your location is one million, three hundred and fifty thousand dollars less than Rogers' location. I'm putting you in charge of the line from here to the summit of the Rockies."

In going over the few miles I had located beyond the gap, Ross thought the line could be improved by crossing the Bow to the east, and back again a few miles further on. We disagreed on this, but he insisted on my trying it. However, after a few days' work he tore up the plans in disgust, saying, "This mountain business is very deceiving. Your line is much the best."

I continued the line west to Devil's Head Creek. Here Rogers' line fol-

3130 SUN DANCE CANYON. BANFF.
R. H. TRUEMAN & CO., PHOTO., VANCOUVE

lowed the Bow River on a long up-grade over a cemented gravel bank; then came a half-mile tunnel through Tunnel Mountain, and a long down-grade to the Bow Valley again. On examination, I found that Tunnel Mountain was an island with a valley to the west of it joining the valley of Devil's Head Creek. So I located the line up this creek and around Tunnel Mountain to the main Bow Valley, shortening the line by a mile, avoiding two long grades and, above all, eliminating the tunnel. On the changed location the heaviest work we encountered was a cut about eight feet deep. The pack trail, over which the engineers must have travelled down many times, zigzagged up over Tunnel Mountain and down again in a series of switch-backs, and I cannot understand why they failed to investigate the valley to the west of it. Rogers' location here was the most extraordinary blunder I have ever known in the way of engineering.

"We sang at times strange melancholy unknown ditties of love."

Morley Roberts, The Western Avernus

We sang at times strange melancholy unknown ditties of love in the forests, songs of Michigan or Wisconsin, redolent of pine odour and sassafras, or German Liede, for we were more cosmopolitan than a crowd of Englishmen would be at home, and did not insist only on what we could understand.

Evenings came to be a recognised institution, and if I felt melancholy or savage one or another of these men would come to the little tent I now had all to myself, and say they wanted me to settle for them some point in dispute. For now, by virtue of my education, which was apparent to them, they made me 'Arbiter elegantiarum,' umpire and referee as to pronunciation, and encyclopaedia, so that I was often hard put to it by a dozen different questions, which only a visit to a library could settle. I wrote for them a song of the C.P.R., or Canadian Pacific Railroad, and all I remember is the chorus, which was—

For some of us are bums, for
 whom work has no charms,
And some of us are farmers, a-
 working for our farms,
But all are jolly fellows, who
 come from near and far,
To work up in the Rockies on the
 C.P.R.

Opposite: Sundance Canyon, Banff, circa 1900;
R.H. Trueman

Cave and Basin, circa 1906; *Elliott Barnes.*

FROM BANFF TO THE GLACIER

Douglas Sladen, On the Cars and Off, 1895

As soon as daylight overtakes you, somewhere on the foot hills round Calgary, a diorama confronts you with a spectacle beside which the Bernese Oberland sinks into insignificance, the long line of the Rocky Mountains, which you have been reading about and dreaming about since you were a child, filling the horizon west and south with a mighty wall, whose battlements are alternate rock and snow. The queer river benches, through which you are passing, rise terrace above terrace, planed off with the geometrical regularity of military earthworks, and, some sixty miles on, you come to the gate of the Rockies—The Gap. Once admitted, and hurling on towards Canmore and Banff, beside the sky-blue river, you see that the wall was no mere illusion of distance, but that the whole range in this part is a castellated formation of an extraordinary beauty, the castellations being picked out with snow.

Mrs. Arthur Spragge, "Our Wild Westland," Dominion Illustrated, Sept 21, 1889

On the morning of July 1st (Dominion Day), which last year fell upon a Sunday, I woke to the beauties of Banff, and, drawing aside the

Banff Springs Hotel, 1888; *Boorne and May.*

curtains of my window, beheld a vision of mountain peaks, off which the mists were slowly rolling. The Banff Springs Hotel faces due north, and my apartment, being in the front, commanded an extensive view across the Bow Valley to the Rockies. An unimproved foreground of ugly stumps, through which the road wound, made an unattractive approach to the building, which, in my humble opinion, should have turned its back to this barren unpromising region and its front to the valleys of the Bow and Spray. It must be remembered, however, that in 1888 the place was yet in its infancy, being only just opened to the public, and, no doubt, the dreary waste between the town and the hotel has since undergone much improvement, as it might be most advantageously laid out in lawns and terraces. When we adjourned to the dining room for breakfast, I discovered that my surmises had been correct, as from that side of the building the best scenery may be enjoyed. The Bow unites with the Spray immediately below the high bluff on which it is situated, the valleys of both rivers being separated by a fine mountain, called from its peculiar formation the Twin Peaks, rising abruptly at their confluence and terminating in a series of bold serrated crags, which

> *"...in 1888 the place was yet in its infancy"*

are sharply defined against the sky.

We sallied forth to contemplate the exterior of the hotel, which we had approached at midnight. It was pronounced by my escort, who is the architect of the Pacific division of the C.P.R., and, therefore, a competent authority, to be in the Schloss style of the Rhenish Provinces, characterised by octagonal towers, with the addition of wide verandahs, having open galleries above. At the ends of two of the wings these galleries are enclosed with glass and form delightful reading and smoking rooms. We decided to descend from the elevation of the hotel to the south valley, and slid and scrambled down a precipitous path to the level of the river, near its junction with the Spray, behind the Banff Springs Hotel. At this point the Bow, which has changed its course a mile above the hotel and taken a southerly bend, tumbles over a pretty fall into a deep dark pool, formed by the backwater from the swiftly flowing current. I soon found a charming view of this cascade, looking northeast directly up the river, which is apparently hemmed in by two noble mountains, round whose bases it winds. I ensconced myself on a block of wood provided by my cavalier, who had rambled across the iron bridge over the Spray to spy out the land beyond.

On these sketching expeditions I feel distinctly and insignificantly an amateur. I travel with neither artist's easel, stool nor umbrella. My outfit is of the simplest, — a sketching block portfolio, a bag containing paint box, water bottle, sponges, wipers, etc.— these, with my own stout gingham, supply my humble needs and proclaim that I am neither ambitious nor professional.

I had not long been at work when my anti-type appeared upon the scene in the person of a vigorous American, who set up an ostentatious easel, seated herself upon the well-known and advertised folding-stool, and erected the protecting umbrella. When a heavy shower drove me temporarily beneath the spreading tree where she was established, I found that she was diligently libelling nature on a vast canvas of good solid oil paint.

Upper Hot Springs, 1907-08; *Elliott Barnes.*

A Mermaid Story

Crag, July 26, 1902

Mr. Franklin B. Helm, of the Molson's bank, Calgary, paid his usual weekly visit to Banff last Saturday and Sunday, and while with a party at Sundance Canyon he wandered away from the crowd and before he could place himself became hopelessly lost in the heavy country around the Sundance. It seems that he must have wandered for hours, for it was late that night when Mr. Helm was found near the Middle Springs and so strong was the afternoon's walk on his nerves that he was, or seemed to be, partly delirious, keeping up a strange conversation about a lot of mermaids he saw. On everything else Mr. Helm was quite rational, but he kept wandering back to the mermaid story and was ready to take his oath that he saw seven or eight mermaids through a large hole in a rock. That they were bathing in a beautiful pool of water and suddenly with strange noises all disappeared through a tunnel in the face of the cave. We all know Mr. Helm is of sound mind, that he is as near to temperance as he can get without wearing the blue and it was some days before we were not quite sure that he had not better be watched. The mystery was cleared up by Mr. Galletly, of the Cave and Basin dropping into our office and asking us to keep a running advertisement in Crag and Canyon to the effect that the ground around the top of the Cave and Basin was sacred.

"eight ladies who were bathing in the Cave complained of a nasty, bold man watching them sporting in the waters of life...."

Why, he said, it was only the other day that seven or eight ladies who were bathing in the Cave, complained of a nasty, bold man watching them sporting in the waters of life.

Mr. Helm was never a confirmed bachelor and we hope that after his late experience we will have the pleasure of putting him in the list of "Hatched, Matched, and Despatched."

Frank now carries a set of opera glasses and swears that next time he will not be fooled easily.

Mrs. Arthur Spragge, "Our Wild Westland," Dominion Illustrated, Sept. 21, 1899

Thither the horses' heads were accordingly turned, and in a short time we drew up at the Lower Hot Spring, which issues from the base of Sulphur Mountain. Its mineral waters are the property of the Dominion Government, who have erected very ornamental and commodious bath-houses, in rustic style, for the convenience of visitors. This spring issues from its source in two entirely distinct ways, offering the peculiarity of both inside and outside natural bathing facilities in hot water. Deep in the bowels of the earth is a large circular grotto enclosing a pool 90 feet in circumference, from whose bottom several springs of very high temperature rise. They are moderated, however, by a stream of cold water that falls from one of the walls and reduces them to a tepid state. This grotto was originally entered through a small opening in its roof, scarcely large enough to admit a man's body, which a ladder connected with the deep pool below. It now serves for purposes of light and ventilation. Another small outlet was subsequently discovered and converted into a tunnel 100 feet long, at present giving access to the interior. The basin of the grotto is lined with concrete, and

Dr. Brett's Sanitarium, a spa described by one visitor as an institution halfway between a grand hotel and a pool room, circa 1890; *Boorne and May.*

The Sanitarium Pharmacy was also called the "Banff Drugstore," John Lawrenceson is the dispenser. A remittance man, whose whiskey she poured down a toilet, called Nurse Mowatt "Rorty Rebecca, the Rat Catcher's Typewriter." In later days she became religiously unbalanced. Nurse McLaughlin is at the right. Circa 1893; *Paris Collection.*

surrounded by a wooden platform, furnished with seats. Taking one of these, I gazed first down into the dark water, then up to the arched vault above, carved by the action of sulphuric forces into every conceivable stalactite and fungoid formation; inhaled brimstony vapours at a temperature of 95 degrees; and fully realised the possible horrors of the Infernal Regions. No more weird or infernal spot could be imagined. A truly Stygian resort, wherein troops of devils might come forth and disport themselves in the dead of night.

Annie White with Jackie, Peter, Lila and their aunt, circa 1910; *Whyte Collection.*

SUMMER GIRL'S LETTER

Crag, August 1, 1903

The hot sulphur baths are wonderful: a deep pool in the rocks with the clearest of green sulphur water, quite warm—and oh! such a delightful sensation it gives you to bathe in it. Then the cave near by! It's worth going miles to see. Mr. Gallantly (or some such name) the dear, old Scotchman who, with lighted lamp, guides you, points out with grief where the stalactites have been knocked off by those "Goths and vandals," the public. He will try to frighten you with wierd stories, and if you do not keep your imagination under control, he will make you believe that you see in one of the peculiarly shaped crevices the skeleton ghost of a noted Indian chief whose imprisonment and death in the cave is said to be part of its earlier history, and then as he leads you out into the bright sunlight again he will tell you lovely romances to make you forget the shudders you had in the mysterious dark.

Yours Affectionately,
Lillian

Douglas Sladen, On the Cars and Off, 1895

The Sanitarium is just outside the town, at the very end of the bridge, over which horses have to proceed at a walk—a maddening way that they have in America to ensure one against the delinquencies of bridge engineers.

Not that the town of Banff is much to boast of. It has a few hundred inhabitants, who have succeeded in making the surrounding woods and mountains more destitute of bird and beast and flower than the Park at Montreal. Though it consists of but a single street, it is horribly over-civilised. It has even a chemist, from whom, as far back as three or four years ago, you could buy Kipling's books in the unauthorised editions published by the Harpers. To make up for this, it has or had a very fine story-teller—the Government Inspector of something or other, to whom Lord Wolseley's successful conduct of the Red River Expedition was apparently due. He had schooled himself for this by destroying whole armies of grizzly bears.

The principal inhabitant at Banff was Dr. Brett, a man of really uncommon energy. He was not only a very clever doctor, whose discovery of the value of Banff Springs had established the fortunes of the town as a summer watering-place; but he had also established the first hotel, the Sanitarium; a livery stable with capital horses for riding and driving; a chemist's shop, both at Banff and Canmore; and was, to boot, Speaker of the Parliament of the North-Western Territories, which meets at Regina.

"...not one of us had ever climbed anything more imposing than little Tunnel, one thousand feet high."

But, with all his energy, he was not so much in evidence as a Canadian Pacific Railway conductor, who was giving himself a week off. This worthy took out a presentation gold watch all day long, and was quite offended because we would not let him "hire a team" and take us out for the day. His only real rival was the man who "had been a gentleman," and now ran the Bow River steamer, a row boat with a wood-fire engine, which took up nearly all the room that was left by the proprietor's sense of importance.

How We Climbed Cascade

Ralph Connor — CAJ, 1907

The main street of Banff runs south to Sulphur mountain, modest, kindly and pine-clad and north to Cascade, sheer, rocky and bare, its great base thrust into the pine forest, its head into the clouds. Day after day the Cascade gazed in steadfast calm upon the changing scenes of the valley below. The old grey face rudely scarred from its age-long conflict with the elements, looked down in silent challenge upon the pigmy ephemeral dwellers of the village at its feet.

It was this calm challenge, too calm for contempt, that moved the Professor to utter himself somewhat impatiently one day, flinging the gauntlet, so to speak, into that stony, immovable face: "We'll stand on your head some day, old man."

We were the Professor by virtue of

his being pedagogue to the town, slight, wiry, with delicate taste for humor; the Lady from Montreal, who, slight as she was and dainty, had conquered Mt. Blanc not long before; the Lady from Winnipeg, literary in taste, artistic in temperament, invincible in spirit; the Man from California, strong, solid and steady; the Lady from Banff, wholesome, kindly, cheery, worthy to be the mother of the three most beautiful babes in all the Park and far beyond it; and the Missionary.

Rock climbing near Banff (part 1), 1903; *Beatrice Longstaff Lance.*

It was a Thursday afternoon in early September of '91, golden and glowing in smoky purple hues. Into a democrat we packed our stuff, provisions for a week, so it seemed, a tent with all necessary camp appurtenances, and started up the valley of the little Forty Mile creek that brawled its stony way from the back of the Cascade. Into the thicker pines, we lost the sunlight; we made our way, dodging trees, crashing through thickets, climbing over boulder masses, till at last the Professor, our intrepid driver, declared that it would be safer to take our team no further. We decided to make this our camp.

By the time the camp was pitched, the pine beds made and supper cooked, darkness had fallen. With appetites sharpened to the danger point, we fell upon the supper and then reclined upon couches of pine, the envy

Rock climbing near Banff (part 2), 1903;
Beatrice Longstaff Lance.

of the immortal gods. With no one to order us to bed, we yarned and sang, indifferent to the passing of the night or to the tasks of the morrow, while the stars slowly swung over our heads.

At last the camp was still. Down the canyon came the long-drawn howl of a wolf, once and again, and we were asleep; the long day and the soothing night proving too much for the shuddering delight of that long, weird, gruesome sound. We turned over in our sleep and woke. It was morning. The Professor was already lighting the breakfast fire. A solid breakfast, prayers, and we stood ready for the climb, greener at our work than the very greenest of the young pines that stood about us, but with fine jaunty courage of the young recruit marching to his first campaign.

An expert mountain-climber, glancing down the line, would have absolutely refused to move from the tent door. With the exception of the Lady from Montreal, who had done Mt. Blanc, not one of us had ever climbed anything more imposing than little Tunnel, one thousand feet high. While as to equipment, we hadn't any, not even an alpenstock between the lot of us. As for the ladies, they appeared to carry their full quota of flimsy skirts and petticoats, while on their feet they wore their second-best kid boots. Without trail, without guide, but knowing that the top was up there somewhere, we set out, water-bottles and brandy-flasks—in case of accident—and lunch baskets slung at the belts of the male members of the party, the sole shred of mountaineering outfit being the trunk of a sapling in the hand of each ambitious climber.

"...the men shall make a half-hour dash for the summit, while the ladies await their return."

Cascade mountain has a sheer face, but a long, sloping back. It was our purpose to get upon that back with all speed. When we considered that we had gone far enough up the valley, we turned sharply and began to climb, finding the slope quite easy and going fairly good.

By 10 o'clock we had got clear of the trees and had begun to see more clearly our direction. But more, we began to realize somewhat more clearly the magnitude of our enterprise. The back of this old Cascade proved to be longer than that bestowed upon most things that have backs, and the lack of equipment was beginning to tell. The ladies of our party were already a grotesquely solemn warning that petticoats and flimsy skirts are not for mountain climbers, and kid boots are better for drawing-rooms.

An hour more, and we began to get views; views so wonderful as to make even the ladies forget their fluttering skirts and clogging petticoats and fast disintegrating boots. We had never imagined there could be so many paths apparently all leading to the mountain top, but we discovered that what had appeared to be an unbroken slope, was gashed by numerous deep gorges that forbade passage, and ever and again we were forced to double on our course and make long detours about these gulches.

By noon the Professor announced, after a careful estimate of distances, that we were more than half way there, and that in an hour's time we should halt for lunch, which double announcement spurred those of the party who had been showing signs of weariness to a last heroic spurt. After lunch the Professor declared that, having been brought up on a farm, he had been accustomed to a noon spell, and must have one. So, stretched upon the broken rocks, we lay disposed at various angles, snuggled down into the soft spots of the old

The Plain of Six Glaciers, below the Victoria Glacier, 1903; *Beatrice Longstaff Lance.*

bony back. We slept for a full half-hour, and woke, so wonderful is this upper air, fresh and vigorous as in the morning. We packed our stuff, passed around our water-bottles, now, alas! almost empty, tied up the bleeding right foot of the Lady from Winnipeg with a portion of the fluttering skirt-remnants of the Lady from Montreal, seized our saplings and once more faced the summit.

Far off a slight ledge appeared directly across our path. Should we make a detour to avoid it? Or was it surmountable? The Professor, supported by the majority of the party, decided for a detour to the left. The Missionary, supported by the Lady from Winnipeg, decided that the frontal attack was possible. In half an hour, however, he found himself hanging to that ledge by his toe-nails and finger-tips, looking down into a gully full of what appeared to be stone, in alpine vocabulary *scree,* and the summit still far above him. Hanging there, there flashed across his mind for a moment the problem as to how the party could secure his mangled remains, and having secured them, how they could transport them down this mountain side. He found himself making a rapid calculation as to the depth of the drop and its effect upon the human frame. Before reaching a conclusion, he had begun edging his way backward, making the discovery that all mountain-climbers sooner or later make, that it is easier to follow your fingers with your toes, than your toes with your fingers.

It is now late in the afternoon, and a council of war is held to decide whether, with all the return journey before us, it is safe to still attempt the peak. We have no experience in descending mountains, and., therefore, we cannot calculate the time required. The trail to the camp is quite unknown to us, and there is always the possibility of accident. The going has become very difficult, for the slope is now one mass of *scree,* so that the whole face of the mountain moves with every step. Still, the peak is very perceptibly nearer, and the party has endured already so much that it is exceedingly loathe to accept defeat. Then, too, the atmosphere has become so rare, that the climbing is hard on the wind, as the Professor says. The ladies, despite shredded skirts and torn shoes, however, are keen to advance, and without waiting for further parley, gallantly strike out for the peak. It is decided to climb for an hour. So up we go, slipping, scrambling, panting, straining ever toward the peak. For an hour and then for half an hour, the ladies still in advance, we struggle upward. The climbing is now over snow and often upon hands and knees, but the *scree* is gone and the rock, where there is no snow, is solid. At length the Professor demands a halt. In spite of desperate

Mt. Lefroy and Mt. Victoria, the Main Ranges, from the summit of Mount Niblock, 1900; *Walter D. Wilcox.*

attempts at concealment, various members of the party are flying flags of distress.

We are still several hundred yards from the coveted summit, but the rose tints upon the great ranges that sweep around are deepening to purple and the shadows lie thick in the valleys. The ladies begin to share the anxiety of the men, knowing full well that it is they who constitute the serious element in the situation. With bitter reluctance they finally decide that they will not ask the men to assume any greater responsibility than they already bear. It is agreed that the men shall make a half-hour dash for the summit, while the ladies await their return. Stripping themselves of all incumbrances, the Professor and the Missionary make a final attempt to achieve the peak, the Californian gallantly offering to remain with the ladies. After a breathless, strenuous half-hour, the Professor, with the Missionary at his side, has fulfilled his threat and accomplished his proud boast. Breathless but triumphant, we are standing upon the head of the old Cascade.

Without a word, we look our fill and turn to the descent. A hundred yards or more and we come upon our party who, with a reckless ambition, have been climbing after us. But the whole back of the Cascade lies now in shadow, and, though half an hour will do it, we dare not encourage them to take the risk. The party has been successful, though individuals have failed. And with this comfort in our hearts and with no small anxiety as to what awaits us, we set off down the slope. It is much easier than we have anticipated until we strike the *scree*. It is here we meet our first accident for the day. The Lady from Winnipeg has the misfortune to turn her ankle. But there is no lack of bandages in the party. In fact, by this time the ladies' skirts consist chiefly of bandages, so that with foot well swathed, and stopping now and then for repairs to the ladies' boots, slipping, sliding, stumbling, leaping, we finally, in a more or less battered condition, arrive at camp.

"...the Professor and I were greatly excited over what appeared to be the fossil remains of a prehistoric monster."

It takes us a full week, the greater part of it spent in bed, to realize that mountain-climbing sans guides, sans mountaineering boots, plus petticoats, is a pastime for angels perhaps, but not for fools.

On the upper part of the mountain, the Professor and I were greatly excited over what appeared to be the fossil remains of a prehistoric monster, and if its jawbone had not weighed several hundred pounds—the backbone must have weighed several tons—we would have carried it down as a present to the Museum. We left them behind us, and they are there to this day for some anthropologist to see.

"Ralph Connor" was the pen name of the Reverend Charles Gordon whose flock was in Banff and Canmore. He is the Missionary in the story he tells above.

Opposite: The Barnes family on the "Green Spot", Stoney Squaw Mountain, circa 1906; *Elliott Barnes.*

Vaux brothers with friends and Swiss Guides on the Victoria Glacier, 1900; *Mary Vaux.*

The Waputehk SnowField

Hugh E.M. Stutfield and J. Norman Collie, Climbs and Explorations in the Canadian Rockies, 1903

A huge crevasse partially covered with snow had to be crossed. All the party had passed over but C.S. Thompson, who unfortunately broke through and at once disappeared headlong into the great crack that ran perpendicularly down into the depths of the glacier. Those of the party who were still on the first peak saw their friends gesticulating in the far distance, but did not take much notice until Peter Sarbach drew their attention to the fact that there were only four people instead of five to be seen: some one therefore, must have fallen down a crevasse. A race across the almost level snow then took place, Sarbach being easily first. Although Thompson was too far down to be seen, yet he could be heard calling for help and saying that, although he was not hurt, he would be extremely grateful to us if

> *"Then he was pushed over the edge of the abyss..."*

Preston L. Tait photographing a crevasse, 1913; *Byron Harmon*

we would make haste and extricate him from the awkward position he was in, for he could not move and was almost upside down, jammed between the two opposing sides of the crevasse.

It was obvious that every second was of importance; a stirrup was made in a rope, and J. Norman Collie, being the lightest member of the party—and, withal, unmarried—was told to put his foot into it, whilst he was also carefully roped round the waist as well. Then he was pushed over the edge of the abyss, and swung in mid-air. To quote his description: "I was then lowered into the gaping hole. On one side the ice fell sheer, on the other it was rather undercut, but again bulged outwards about eighteen feet below the surface, making the crevasse at that point not much more than two feet wide. Then it widened again, and went down into dim twilight. It was not till I had descended sixty feet, almost the whole available length of an eighty foot rope, that at last I became tightly wedged between the two walls of the crevasse, and was absolutely incapable of moving my body. My feet were close to Thompson's but his head was further away, and about three feet lower than his heels. Face downwards, and cov-

Mary Vaux at the Illecillewaet Glacier, 1899; *Vaux collection.*

ered with fallen snow, he could not see me. But, after he had explained that it was entirely his own fault that he was there, I told him we would have him out in no time. At the moment I must say I hardly expected to be able to accomplish anything. For, jammed between two slippery walls of ice, and only able to move my arms, cudgel my brains as I would, I could not think what was to be done. I shouted for another rope. When it came down I managed to throw one end to Thompson's left hand, which was waved about, till he caught it. But, when pulled, it merely dragged out of his hand. Then with some difficulty I managed to tie a noose on the rope by putting both my hands above my head. With this I lassoed that poor pathetic arm which was the only part of Thompson that could be seen. Then came the tug-of-war. If he refused to move, I could do nothing more to help him; moreover, I was afraid that at any moment he might faint. If that had occurred I do not believe he could have been got out at all, for the force of the fall had jammed him further down than it was possible to follow. Slowly the rope tightened, as it was cautiously pulled by those above. I could hear my heart thumping in the ghastly stillness of the place, but at last Thompson began to shift, and after some short time he was pulled into an upright position by my side. To get a rope round his body was of course hopeless. Partly by wriggling and pulling on my own rope I was so shifted that by straining one arm over my head I could get my two hands together, and then tied the best and tightest jamming knot I could think of round his arm, just above the elbow. A shout to the rest of the party, and Thompson went rapidly upwards till he disappeared

Illecillewaet Glacier, August 11, 1899; *Vaux Collection.*

Edward Feuz Sr., Fred Michel, Charles Clarke, and Karly Schluneggar, circa 1901; *R.H. Trueman*

round the bulge of ice forty feet or more above. I can well remember the feeling of dread that came over me lest the rope should slip or his arm give way under the strain, and he should come thundering down on the top of me; but he got out all right, and a moment later I followed. Most marvellously no bones had been broken, but how any one could have fallen as he did without being instantaneously killed will always remain a mystery. He must have partially jammed some considerable distance higher up than the point where I found him, for he had a rück-sack on his back, and this perhaps acted as a brake, as the walls of the crevasse closed in lower down. We were both of us nearly

Locomotive for the tour of the Governor-General, Lord Stanley of Preston, October 1889; *Boorne and May.*

frozen and wet to the skin, for ice-cold water was slowly dripping the whole time on us; and in my desire to be as little encumbered as possible, I had gone down into the crevasse very scantily clad in a flannel shirt and knickerbockers."

A rapid descent to the head of the ice-fall quickly restored circulation, and that night over the camp fire the whole experience was gone over again, Thompson emphatically giving it as his opinion that, whatever scientific exploration or observation in future might be necessary on the summits of the Rocky Mountains, investigations made alone, sixty feet below the surface of the ice, in an inverted position, were extremely dangerous and even unworthy of record.

Pauline Todd and Alice Harding, sisters, circa 1914; *Harding Collection.*

Glacier House decorated in honour of the Duke and Duchess of Cornwall and York, 1901; *R.H Trueman*

Morley Roberts, On the Old Trail, 1927

Presently we came to the derelict hotel in a very beautiful situation. Once the railroad passed it, sweeping in a mighty curve round the head of the valley. The great new Connaught Tunnel, put through in 1913, has done away with this part of the rail. Glacier House is, in its architectural character, far more suited to its forest and mountain surroundings than the great hotels of the Rockies.

The way to the Glacier is up no rude forest trail but over well-made paths and bridges. A more beautiful walk it is impossible to conceive. Sometimes it reminded me of the Gorges du Chaudron and then of half-forgotten ramblings about Zermatt. The young Illicilliwaet comes roaring down from the glaciers up above, the Great Glacier itself and the even more imposing glacier system of Asulkan, which sends down a great tributary.

As we had met no one after leaving the hotel we were alone just under the glacier. This solitude fitted the gloom of the day: I should have been sorry to see crowds of tourists there. I do not know how many of them come merely to say they have seen the place, but probably the percentage is not small. One man we met in the Rockies de-

clared that he met a heavy elderly woman from the United States who asked him how far the Glacier was. As she was wearing high heels and was over-dressed and visibly perspiring he took pity upon her. "Why, ma'am, it's a long way yet and not worth seeing. The four train loads of ice that the Company brings up every year haven't yet arrived!" She heaved a sigh of relief and turned back.

AT THE SUMMIT OF THE SELKIRKS

A.O. Wheeler, "Rogers Pass at the Summit of the Selkirks," CAJ, 1929

Glacier House, a delightful mountain resort, soon became famous and additions were necessary to supply the demand for accommodation. A very charming and efficient lady, Mrs. J.M. Young, was made manager. Two distinct qualities stood out: a keen sense of humour and a sympathetic interest in all with whom she came in contact. She was lovingly known to those around her as "Mother Young," and all, from the highest plutocrat among her guests to the lowliest section man of the railway service, brought their needs and woes to her, to be met with ready sympathy and a humourous smile, and many of the needs were supplied from her own resources. Her particularly keen sense of humour furnished an endless supply of anecdotes culled chiefly from the idiosyncrasies of her guests.

"My dear Madam, the bed is not in the magnetic meridian."

A fine-looking old gentleman registered at the hotel and was given a room. Shortly after, he appeared at the office in a state of great excitement. "Madam! I cannot sleep in that room." "Why?" asked Mrs. Young, "it is one of our best." "My dear Madam, the bed is not in the magnetic meridian." "Well!" replied Mrs. Young, "can you not put it there?" "Oh, may I?" "Certainly; you can put it outside the window, if you like." And he went off quite happy, with his little pocket compass, to put his bed in the magnetic meridian.

Then there was the young midshipman who was on his way to Hong Kong. Mrs. Young was wakened in the

Opposite: Mary Vaux and Swiss Guides on Asulkan Pass, looking at Mount Dawson and the Fox Glacier, July 14, 1900; *Vaux Collection.*

middle of the night by the violent ringing of his room bell. Thinking someone was sick, she went to see. On opening the door, she discovered a wild-eyed youth in pyjamas who could only exclaim: "My tickets! My tickets!" Having calmed him down and extracted an explanation, she found that his railway and steamboat tickets, supplied him by the British Admiralty, were in one of the pockets of his tennis flannels sent that day to the laundry. Mrs. Young forthwith went to the laundry and retrieved the tennis flannels, and, sure enough, the tickets, reduced to a ball of pulp in the washing, were in one of the trouser pockets. Thanks to Mrs. Young's good offices and those of Mr. Tom Kilpatrick, Superintendent of the Mountain Division of the Railway, matters were promptly straightened out and the youth sent of his way rejoicing.

I was once camped at Albert Canyon, close beside the station. My men were busy loading a pack-train to go farther afield. Suddenly an express train crowded with passengers from the Orient rushed in and stopped directly opposite my camp. In a moment all was wildest confusion. The horses became unmanageable, reared on their hind legs and careered around with men swearing frantically and trying to hold them. One horse broke away, dashed into the brush, leaped a log four feet high, burst its cinches and scattered its pack to the four winds. The people on the train, who had been thoroughly enjoying the miserable spectacle, clapped their hands, waved their handkerchiefs and shouted "encore."

A log book was also opened and was a joy to read. The unbiased sentiments of those who braved the terrors of the surrounding peaks with the Swiss guides stationed at the chalet were most confiding. One entry in particular appealed to me. It had reference to the climatic conditions at the Selkirks' summit during the latter part of the summer, which, to put it mildly, are somewhat variable. The entry was by a disappointed climber who had waited a long time to make the ascent of Mt. Sir Donald. It read as follows:

First it rained, and then it snew,
  and then it friz, and
then it thew, and then it fogged,
  and the it blew,
  and very shortly after then,
it rained and snew
and friz and thew
and fogged and blew

Phimister Proctor painting on the shore of Maligne Lake, 1911; *Byron Harmon.*

A.O. Wheeler, "Roger Pass at the Summit of the Selkirks," CAJ, 1929

The first ascent of Mt. Sir Donald by a lady was made by Mrs. E. E. Berens, of Kent, England, on her honeymoon. The important question was what should she wear for the occasion. A council of war was held by the ladies at the hotel, and it was decided that a pair of her husband's knickerbockers was the proper thing. She naturally chose his best pair, and was surprised several times during the day to find herself holding them up by a finger and thumb as though it had been a skirt. Such a thing would not occur now-a-days. Her remarks in the log book were indicative of wisdom: "Be wise, friends, and do not despise a mountain; it always gets the better of you in the end... In climbing, look for the next hand and foothold and nothing more, for if you look down it is apt to frighten you and if you look up you get discouraged."

An Artist's Reminiscences

F.M. Bell-Smith

CAJ, 1918

In the year 1888, while staying at Glacier House, I was invited by the Rev. W. S. Green to accompany him on a visit to Corbin's Mine. I gladly accepted the kind invitation, in spite of some misgivings as to my ability to keep up with such climbers on the ascent of four thousand feet. When we arrived at Illecillewaet, from which point the trail started, I found horses all ready, and the sight filled me with a new sensation of which, however, I was careful not to betray any visible sign. *I had never ridden a horse in my life.* To my astonishment I got on better than I expected, for by watching very closely the others mount, and doing as nearly as I could like them, I was in the saddle before I realized it.

Clouds on Mt. Robson, 1913; *Byron Harmon.*

We started, and the trail led through thick forest for over two hours without anything to see, and I began to wonder if I should have felt any more tired if I had walked. But I was afraid to dismount as some did for a rest and change, being far from sure that on a steep trail I could get on again as easily as I had done at the start. At length we reached tree line, and soon commenced to cross a very steep slope, so steep that I had difficulty in keeping my left foot from striking the bank, while on my right it seemed as though I could look straight down. No doubt this was an exaggerated impression, but Mr. Corbin seemed to consider this a sort of "test" place, for turning to me—he being the leader, and I second in the line—he told me of people who had been over this spot who shut their eyes and clasped their horse round the neck in terror, and he seemed rather surprised when he no-

Byron Harmon filming the Illecillewaet Valley, circa 1920.

lead; and that on one occasion when they were at the exact spot to which we were then coming my animal attempted to pass the mule, and rolled down over a thousand feet, escaping with the loss of one eye.

I was deeply impressed by this story, and was glad enough when we passed the place.

The mine being about sixteen hundred feet down on the other side of the pass, we all dismounted and rested long enough for me to make a sketch before we descended to the mine.

That evening after supper, Mr. Corbin was good enough to volunteer some rather complimentary remarks upon my Horsemanship and, when I very modestly admitted that I had never ridden on any animal with four legs in my life until that day, I am convinced that he considered me to be either a joker or a liar.

While stopping at Glacier House in 1899 I secured the studies for my painting, "The Heart of the Selkirks."

ticed that I was unconcernedly looking at the river four thousand feet below.

He then asked me if I had observed the fact of my horse having only one eye, and proceeded to give me a minute account of how he lost it. He explained that between my beast—a sort of Cayuse with an evil look in his one eye—and the mule he was riding there existed a strong rivalry for the

CPR rotary snowplough, circa 1890; *Boorne and May.*

The point of view is known as "Avalanche Crest," said to be three thousand or more feet above the hotel and reached by a good trail for about three-quarters of the distance, after which it is a bit of a scramble up a steep slippery grassy slope to the crest of an arête from which the view is very fine. To this point I climbed three times in one week, being turned back on the first attempt when only a short distance from the top by what looked like a furious storm, but which, after driving my guide and me back, switched into another valley and cleared off. The second time I went alone, and had just reached the rocky wall, fifty feet or so below the crest, when a storm did come in good earnest. Quickly divesting myself of as much clothing as possible, and caching it under a rock, I scrambled up in the teeth of the driving rain, and climbing over the crest stood up and took my ducking like a shower bath. For half an hour or more it continued to pour, and then for a long time the clouds blotted out everything. But I waited, and shivered, and waited. By and by there was an opening —yes, there, through a rift, the sun was shining on the Asulkan Glacier. More rifts, and then all closed up again, then more, and more rifts, and the—oh, wonders! Such a sight as

> *"...I had never ridden a horse in my life."*

Ken Liddell,
I'll Take the Train

Sixty-four men were buried alive at Summit. They had been clearing the tracks of one slide when a second covered them, left some of them standing corpses under 50 feet of snow. They were covered so quickly that one man was found with his arms upraised and solid in death, a plug of tobacco in one hand, a knife in the other. He was completing an act that would have filled the pipe that was in his mouth.

Testing the bearing strength of the Stony Creek steel bridge which replaced the original pile bridge, 336 feet in span, 295 feet high, 1893.

I can never forget. I jumped and shouted in my excitement. The clouds were rising from the valley in long festoons, the sun, lighting up glaciers and snow fields and breaking in gleams through the fast diminishing clouds, produced such a scene as would out-do anything I ever saw in a moving picture show.

I came up to get a sketch of the panorama! That was impossible, there were only fleeting glimpses and the constant shifting of the clouds made sketching impossible. I could only take out my book, which I had tucked somewhere under my arm to keep from the rain, and make a few notes in pencil. But the impression made was so vivid and eneffaceable, that I was able to make what many consider to be my best painting of a mountain subject.

Bow River and Twin Peaks (Mt. Rundle), circa 1900; *R.H. Trueman*

AN OLD-TIMER'S PLAINT

Crag, Aug. 14, 1909

To the Editor of "Crag and Canyon"

SIR—The world can stand still for no one, and yet the pace at which the old sphere has been running—along the C.P.R. line—for the past year or two has been an eye-opener to one who has visited your little town and other stopping places along the road in the past. Tom Wilson, Bill Peyto and Bob Campbell were familiar names to all who loved the cayuse's back and the smell of the camp fire. Where are they today? Who knew so well how to throw the diamond hitch, fry a pan of bacon, make a bough bed, or tell fascinating yarns when the day's march or hunt was over? We find but a handful of the old men left, the men who have

James Irving "Jim" Brewster, circa 1905.

Corckscrew Drive, Banff, circa 1915; *Byron Harmon.*

dug deep into the secrets of camp life and with their own strong personalities lured us from the stockmarkets, the exchanges, the rush of business life in the east to forget for a time our cares by living with men who knew how to live?

Your mountains and rivers remain, but after a few years—only a few—I come among you again to find myself escorted over your Banff roads by a driver who does not know Mt. Rundle from Cascade; to be sent to Lake O'Hara in the care of a boy who can't fry bacon or tie on a pack, and "didn't know that mountains had names."

At Field and Glacier I was cheered by the sight of three real, bona fide outfitters, with live, well-fed, well-trained animals, who knew me and could talk the language of the trail, and it warmed my heart to find a spot in the old hills where the almighty tourist dollar had not choked out all humanity to the horse, and where I could find something to ride that conscience permitted me so to do. Wake up, you people of Banff; wake up, my old friend C.P.R.

We people of the east have known the very cream of camping in your country. You are giving us some very false coin in return for our loyalty. Bring to the front the real, the reliable outfitter, and send back to town the youngsters who in stage "shaps" pose as wild cowboys to the innocent and unsuspecting tourist.

Yours, &c.,
Disgusted

On Tunnel Mountain, August 5, 1903; *Beatrice Longstaff Lance.*

Walter D. Wilcox, The Rockies of Canada, 1909

A crowd of the business men of Banff, who usually take about 365 holidays every year, stands around to offer advice and watch the sport. Then the picturesque train of horses with their wild-looking drivers files out through the village streets under a fusillade of snap-shot cameras and the wondering gaze of new arrivals from the east.

Crag, Sept. 26, 1908

The drivers of the local livery barns have many a good story to tell of their experiences with "green" tourists. One which we heard lately was of a lady who, after exhausting the usual stock of "fool" questions, insisted on the driver stopping the rig in order to allow her to get out and stroke a porcupine that was meandering down the road. Fortunately for the nature lover, the "porky" did not wait to be petted.

AIRSHIP STATION ON CASCADE MT.

Crag, Aug. 28, 1909

The following appeared in the Calgary "Herald" of Thursday, and is of such importance locally that we reproduce it for the benefit of our readers: —

Calgary has the distinction of being the home of the first airship station company in the Dominion of Canada. Clifford T. Jones, barrister, of this city,

Dave White's store, circa 1911, his children sitting on the sidewalk; *Whyte Collection.*

has made application to Commissioner of Parks Howard Douglas, at Banff, for the lease of 500 feet of the top of Cascade mountain. The ultimate object is to have a station for airships on the premises.

Mr. Jones and various clients are at present negotiating the formation of a company, and although they recognise that it is yet a little early for airship erections, nevertheless they are satisfied that within a very few years locations will be necessary, and they consider the top of Cascade mountain to be an ideal site for the purpose.

In addition to the ultimate object, the peak could be made very useful for mountain climbing, etc.

Of course a station will also be built in Banff proper, and tourists and others who wished could make the trip to the peak, which has an elevation of 10,000 feet. The view from the top is said to be most magnificent, showing numerous lakes, valleys and streams of the Rockies, and on clear days, Mr. Jones says, even Calgary can be seen in the distance.

The promoter is enthusiastic over the scheme, and considers it a very plausible one, and has no doubt of its future success. The application has been forwarded to Ottawa, but as the matter is rather out of the ordinary it may be some time before a reply is received.

Danish Pastry chef, circa 1923; *Byron Harmon.*

Bring on the Dance

Crag, June 29, 1907

We are pleased to publish the following clever poem from the pen of a Banff gentleman, whose modesty will not allow the use of his name:

"Bring on the Dance;
Let Mirth be Free."
Once in a crowded ball-room
Of Banff's exclusive set,
I saw a thing that shocked,
And caused me much regret.
It was a "masher," and a lady
Endowed with every charm,
Who flirted; now don't tell me
That that was any harm.
Not when the lady's free to wed;
But oh! Upon my life!
'Tis different when the fair one is
Another party's wife.
For husbands are not always blind,
And oft times make things hum,
When in between the marriage band
A blighter dares to come.
This fellow's cheeks were rosy red
(Sam Scott's man does it well),
And with red hair to match the cheek
Made quite a howling swell.
With low-cut dress and sprightly air,

The Lady of the Cake, circa 1912; *Byron Harmon.*

The fair one floated on;
Whilst round her waist the masher's arm
Safe guided through the throng.
Now as her glistening shoulders flashed
Beneath the lights strong glare,
The masher boldly pressed a kiss
Upon her shoulders bare.
This is not all by any means,
As others there can tell;
But more just now I will not say
For fear of raising well.
As other eyes have watched this game
Dear reddy, please beware,
Lest some fine day your "Mashing Bouts"
May be ended in black despair.
Your smoke don't cover all the land,
Despite your ruddy glow;
Be wise and put your cap on straight,
And go a trifle slow.
Don't think in telling this nice tale
I've shot my only "bolt,"
Some other day I yet may give
Your nerve another jolt.
Ye husbands all, don't wander far
While mischief may be done;
Keep one eye on this masher red,
And the other on your gun.

John Walker in front of his store, 1897. Either John Walker or Mr. Galletly were caretakers at the Cave and Basin, depending on which political party was in power in Ottawa.

Crag, July 27, 1907

The most talked of woman in the United States, Mrs. Evelyn Thaw, with her mother and some friends, are staying at the Banff Springs Hotel this week. The party are strictly incog., but the publicity given the chief characters in the nauseous trial makes identification easy.

Closing of the Tourist Season

By D. C. Bayne

Crag, Sept. 27, 1902

We have heard the question asked, "Where do the majority of the tourists come from?" We have no statistics at hand by which we can frame a definite answer, but we venture the opinion from personal observation that the cities of the eastern and northern States send the largest quota, while Great Britain may lay claim to a good second place.

Many Canadians visit Banff, but the average Canadian has neither the time nor the wealth to be classed as a tourist. Banff has the distinction of being the most cosmopolitan place in Canada.

We have had visitors from every part of the civilized world. The polished Frenchman; the stolid Teuton, the energetic American; the lordly Englishman; the hardy and canny Scot; the ruddy son of Erin's isle; the citizen

Dr. R.G. Brett with some of his Sanitarium staff, circa 1900; *George Paris.*

of the South African veldt; the sunbrowned Australian; the East Indian and even the heathen Oriental, have at one time or another during the past summer been to Banff, and of all these we have never heard of one who was not charmed with Banff and its surroundings.

> *"Banff has the distinction of being the most cosmopolitan place in Canada."*

Crag, June 29, 1907

On Monday there was a car-load of tourists turned loose on Banff that certainly took the cake for original and unbecoming costumes. They were from one of the eastern cities, and the ladies had evidently studied the pictures of Miss Peck, the champion lady mountaineer, and modelled their costumes on hers. Short stout women in knee skirts and leggings and tall thin ones in the same unbecoming rigout, paraded the streets, and some of the more venturesome of them made the ascent of Tunnel Mountain. They were on their way to the coast, where they intend to "conquer" the easy slopes of Mount Rainier, and on their way are apparently breaking in their new togs.

This must have been taken about 1895. I wasn't old enough to go to school. My mother and I were up from Morley and staying at Wilson's. Mrs. Wilson had just had Bessie, and with four other kids couldn't cope with everything. The Wilsons lived next door to the School. In this picture you will see May Jack, Ada Wilson, Pearl Brewster with a kid eating the rim off her hat, Harper Wellman, Fred Brewster, Jack and Gypsy Harper, their father was in charge of the R.M.P., John Wilson... and sitting on the ground Fred Cobb, George Brewster, I am the little one in front with my hand up to my mouth. I had a ring with a stone in it, and when I knew the picture was going to be taken, I ran into the house to get the ring. The photographer said he would be back next day to take another, and for us to be dressed up so...

Crag, May 19, 1906

Work begins this morning on the cutting of the trenches for the water and sewerpipes through the streets and avenues of the town by the steam digger. The machine is a large one, weighing 28 tons, and is propelled by a 27 h.p. engine, while the force working the digger is of 112 h.p., or four h.p. to each ton of weight. The work will commence just north of the Bow bridge, and it is hoped that Buffalo street corner will be passed at an early hour, so as to leave the approach to the bridge clear for horse traffic, which it will be advisable to keep off that portion of the main avenue where the machine is being used. The Buckeye Trac-

... here we are the next day. Pearl didn't make it, Mr. Walker was passing by so he got into the picture as did a policeman. My mother was hanging out clothes, so she was also called. I now wonder if in those days they wore hats when they put the clothes out? In the picture you will also see May Jack, Mrs. Fulmer, Fulmer children, (where are the twins now??), Fred Cobb, Harper Wellman, the Harpers, Ada Wilson, Rene Wilson peeking out from behind me, Eddie at my feet, another little boy, and George Brewster. Wasn't Mr. Jones tall and straight? – *Maud Kidney*

tion Ditcher is the name of the machine, which cuts to a perfect grade, passing over the ground but once, and working in soft or hard ground, and when the ground is frozen, being able to cut through anything not requiring blasting. The employment of this powerful implement will hasten the much desired completion of the task of furnishing the Sulphur City with the most essential conveniences of modern civilisation. The turning on of the water cannot come too soon for some householders, as we have heard of several wells in which the supply of water is approaching the vanishing point.

"Cowboys and Indians," behind the Alberta Hotel, 1914; *Moore Collection.*

Constable Drane Disappears

Crag, Aug 24, 1907

The records of the R.N.W.M.P. were stained this week when Constable Drane, of the local detachment, vamoosed, skipped out, levanted, hiked, or otherwise got away from Banff, leaving no permanent (or temporary) address. To add to the distress occasioned by this sudden departure, it was found, after he had gone, that the dog tax for 1907 had been collected, but not turned in to the Government office, and Drane is supposed to have forgotten to leave it when preparing to hit the trail. Drane was a well-liked young fellow who is well connected, and this lapse from the paths of honesty is much regretted; but the blame is not entirely to be placed on his shoulders. He was only a young fellow, and naturally followed the lead set by others, and the pace was too rapid for a constable's pay. Corporal Browning, who was Drane's superior, should have kept a closer tab on Drane, and reduced the temptation to use other people's money to a minimum.

What the townspeople said when they heard the news:

Hair on him.
Wouldn't that jar you.
How did he stand IT as long as he did.
His ways were not our ways.
It was the wrong one.
I wonder if my dog tax will be collected again.
Did Drane really take it?
The police are rotten.
Bang goes my four 'n arf dollars.

North West Mounted Police Barracks, Banff, circa 1888.

Thief Caught

no source provided

Mrs. Ferguson, of Calgary, who a short time ago lost some jewelry out of her room in one of the down-town hotels, has had the greater part of it returned through the efforts of Chief English, of Calgary, who had the thief arrested in Vancouver. This case was reported to the Banff police at once, yet the thief got clear away, to let the chief of police of Calgary carry off the honors of securing him.

Summer resorts are as a rule the pasture lands of petty thieves, and the past summer in Banff has been no exception to the rule. A great deal of petty thieving has occurred here this summer, and ALWAYS to the profit of the sneak thief. It is sure time for a change, as the police in Banff are little better than useless.

Flitting of Mrs. Brown

Crag, July 25, 1908

Mrs. Brown, who ran Brown's restaurant and Banff restaurant, made a moonlight flitting last Friday night, leaving behind a host of unpaid bills in Banff and Calgary. The total amount of furniture, etc. left for the creditors will not amount to any more than will settle the rent bills and give the help a small portion of their wages, while other claims, amounting to about $1,500, will have to be written off by the creditors to profit and loss.

From what can be learned, it would seem as if the move had been contemplated for some time, as she had a large sum in cash in her possession when she left, and had been putting off her creditors with excuses for the past few weeks.

The getaway was made by Mr. and Mrs. Brown and the children driving to Canmore, and there selling the horse and boarding the evening train for the east. They were located at Fort William at the instance of the R.N.W.M.P., but were allowed to proceed. When overhauled at Fort William, tickets for England were found in their possession, and they doubtless are on the high seas ere now.

> *"The first hymn sung was appropriately, "Upon the mountain we meet Thee, my God."*
> *Salvation Army knee drill on Tunnel Mt., August, 1909.*

ORLANDO WAS PINCHED

Crag, Aug. 14, 1909

Thomas Wilfred Orlando Walters was evidently much enamoured of souvenirs, for last weekend he was in the Sign of the Goat Store and helped himself to the curios he felt he needed, and left without paying. But T.W. Orlando etc. was of a generous mould, and made a present of a cigar case to one of the moisture vendors at the Hotel King Edward, where the many named was staying. Thus N.K.L. got wise, and when Corpl. Ryan looked into the trunks of Orlando he found many souvenirs which had not been purchased. So Orlando was gathered to the police cells, and the J.P. sent him down to Calgary for two month's hard.

A FEW THINGS THAT NEED FIXING OR ARE WANTED

Crag, May 6, 1911

A first-class dentist in Banff.
The Upper Hot Springs bath house.
Bow Bridge at Banff.
Cinder walks on side streets.
The roads outside of the village.
The Foreman of the Park.
Freehold tenure for village lots.
An advisory board to check some of the stunts the people are getting handed to them.
A steam road roller.
A new Minister of the Interior.
A live agent to make Banff a Winter Resort.
A big pavilion for music in the summer and curling in the winter.

Arthur Saddington, Ralph Edwards, Bill Mather, curling on the Bow River backwater, 1898; *George Paris.*

Crag, May 6, 1911

The main street of Banff has taken on its summer appearance and the road has been raked free of stones from the bridge to the school house.

W.A. Griesbach, I Remember, 1946

In an election for the Provincial Legislature it was agreed that at a certain place, near Banff, a joint meeting would be held between the candidates. That is to say both candidates would appear on the platform at the same time and place, dividing the time between them. Arthur Sifton arrived on time but Dr. Brett as usual was late. After sitting around for some time, the audience began to get restive and the chairman addressing the meeting suggested that they might as well have Mr. Sifton's speech now and Dr. Brett could speak when he arrived. This was not quite the arrangement which the audience had expected. They wanted to see both candidates in action facing each other. Sifton, however, was willing, took the platform and made his speech and sat down. Still Brett did not arrive and again the audience began to get restive. Sifton then got up and addressing the chairman pointed out that he and Dr. Brett had been campaigning all over the constituency and probably knew each other's speeches by heart and since Dr. Brett had not arrived he was quite willing to deliver Dr. Brett's speech. This met with the approval of the audience and Sifton, who had a sardonic wit, then delivered Dr. Brett's speech. Sifton had no sooner finished Brett's speech than Brett arrived all smiles and bows to everybody and took his seat on the platform. Thereupon the chairman called on him to speak. As the audience recognized the parts of Brett's speech that Sifton had already delivered on his behalf there were howls of delight from the audience.

Mixed hockey, Mather's rink, Bow River, 1906-07; *Elliott Barnes.*

TEN WORDS OF COLD TYPE

Crag, Sept. 2, 1911

"R.B." held his little "talk fest" in the Brett Opera House last Wednesday evening. Arrayed in a "claw hammer" and displaying a diamond pin of such a "caratage" that it pulled him over in front into that ingratiating position so suited for the diffusion of soft soap, he took the hobbles off that mellifluous voice which is the pride of Conservative Calgary.

To hear Mr. Bennett once is to hear him all the time. He expands his Websterian chest and gives tongue to the same old platitudes about "our noble land," "this great heritage of ours," etc., ad infinitum, ad nauseum, which he introduces into every speech, whether political, after dinner, or pleading for the life of the C.P.R. before the beak.

Even the most rabid Conservative cannot help admitting that the meeting was a frost. The "Old Guard" of the local Conservatives rallied around their Cambronne and the curtain was rung up on the last act of their Waterloo.

Mr. Bennett side-stepped issues with all the grace and agility of a Spanish matador. It is not so much what he says as what he does not say or insinuates. When asked if he was still in the employ of the C.P.R. he did not have the nerve to come out with a good square "No", but lawyer-like remarked "Mr. Walker took over my duties on the first of last May!" How is that for dodging? It is a good bet that he will be back on the same old job after the 21st ready to plead his cases at "the foot of the throne."

Edward, Prince of Wales, with Dr. R.G. Brett, who had become the Lieutenant-Governor of Alberta, 1919; *Whyte Collection.*

Crag, Aug. 3, 1912

The dismissing of Howard Douglas, Chief Superintendent of Dominion Parks, is announced from Ottawa. The cause given is offensive partisanship during the Dominion elections of September 1911; but up to the present no details of any wrongdoing on the part of Mr. Douglas have been given out. The public will be curious to know why it took the Government nearly a year to dispense with Mr. Douglas's services if the circumstances were of such a nature as to warrant his dismissal by wire. It would be difficult to convince reasonable people that Mr. Douglas's dismissal was due to any other fact than that some supporter of the present administration in Ottawa coveted his position. His dismissal is yet another example of the pernicious effect of the spoils system in the good government of the country.

During his tenure of office as Superintendent of the Banff National Park, from 1897 to 1909—a period of 11 years—Mr. Douglas did everything in his power to improve the condition of the Park in the interests not only of the Government, but of the people. He was closely in touch with existing conditions and invariably fought hard for the remedy of existing grievances. As Chief Superintendent of Dominion Parks, he did excellent work.

Ike Brooks Makes Record Ride

Over Mountain Trails to secure a Doctor for his Suffering Daughter

Crag, Dec. 4, 1915

Ike Brooks, who has an enviable reputation as an all-around mountaineer and broncho buster, has proved that he is of the stuff heroes are made of.

He lives, with his family, on the Little Red Deer and last week his daughter, aged about 16, was taken suddenly ill with all the symptoms of appendicitis.

Ike saddled a horse and set out for Olds, a distance of some ninety miles. Securing the services of a physician, he at once started on the return journey without pausing for a moment's rest. At Sundre about 25 miles from the ranch the Olds sawbones developed an acute attack of "cold feet" and refused to go any farther.

"...260 miles of mountain trails, with only an hour's sleep and mighty little to eat."

Pushing on to his ranch alone, Ike found that his daughter was no better. Pausing only long enough to eat a hurried meal he started for Banff, making the journey with one horse through snow eight feet deep in places.

With a scant hour's rest, while Dr. Atkin was making necessary preparations, Brooks and the doctor started on the return journey to the Brooks ranch.

After Ike left Sundre, Wm. McCue, forest ranger, called up the Olds physician and put the case up to him so foribly (sic) that he consented to answer the call. He went to Coal Camp, 35 miles, by auto, 25 miles in a rig and the remaining 20 miles on horseback. During the last stretch he fell in a river and was hauled out with a rope over a saddle horn. He remained at the ranch four or five hours, until Dr. Atkin arrived, then went to Logan's camp, lost himself while out hunting and it required the entire staff of forest rangers to locate and bring him in. (It is a pleasure to give the Olds doctor all the credit coming to him in this case.)

Dr. Atkin and Ike met trouble with a big T on their way to the ranch. They left Banff at midnight and rode along mountain trails, dangerous going in summer time, plunging through snow drifts and picking their way over frozen water. While crossing a mountain stream the doctor's horse broke through the ice, plunged and fell with its rider buried underneath in the icy waters. By the time Ike got the horse off him and he had rolled out of the water Atkin was some damp, but he took a pull at a flask of hooch, grinned and said "Lead on, Ike, I'll follow you," climbed into the saddle and rode several miles in his dripping garments until a camp shack was reached and he had an opportunity to strip and dry his clothing around a blazing fire. Ike says the doctor nev-

A snowshoer above Johnston Canyon, circa 1924; *Byron Harmon.*

er grumbled during the entire ride of 22 hours, notwithstanding the fact that he was unused to such strenuous exercise, he just kept a coming. Dr. Atkin operated upon the patient as soon as her condition would permit and remained for several days watching the case.

Nurse Fulcher was another Banffite who "played the game." She made the trip from here to Olds by train, to Logan's camp by auto and two-wheeled cart. Arriving there in the middle of the night she was still game to go on and make the last 20 miles on horseback, reaching the ranch at five o'clock in the morning with undiminished energy but a weary body. The trail in winter would test the endurance of a mountaineer, but she never faltered during the 29 hour journey.

It is such prompt and unfaltering response to the call of duty that has gained the medical fraternity of Banff the enviable reputation they enjoy.

Upon reaching his home Brooks had ridden 260 miles of mountain trails, with only an hour's sleep and mighty little to eat.

It is such feats of pluck and endurance that have made the dwellers among the Rockies the big men they are, and proves that all heroic deeds are not performed in the limelight.

Crag, Dec. 18, 1915

Ike Brooks was in from the Brewster ranch on the Big Red Deer last Friday night with the information that his daughter had been successfully operated upon by Dr. Atkin and was making a nice recovery under the watchful care of Nurse Fulcher.

A CHRISTMAS TREK

CAJ, 1909

Tom Wilson's home is at Banff, but his business of horse-ranching takes him for a large part of the year to the Kootenai Plain, on the North Saskatchewan, where his ranch is situated. Some little time before last Christmas Day he started from his ranch to celebrate the annual festival with his family at Banff.

> *"wood had to be collected and cut to keep alive during the night..."*

"There is not much to tell of my trip over the Pipestone Pass. It was simply the case of a man starting on a seventy-mile snowshoe trip across the mountains to eat his Christmas dinner with his wife and family, and of getting there and eating the dinner, the pleasure being well worth the trip. I rode to within eight miles of the summit and started early the next morning on snowshoes to cross the pass (8,300 feet alt.). It was snowing a little and very cold when I started, and when I got opposite the Clearwater Gap a blizzard came up, and I could not see more than six or eight feet ahead in the grey snow light that makes everything look level. I was on the trail along the mountain side, and was afraid of falling down one of those steep side collars (which you will remember on that side), and of breaking my snowshoes, so I turned and went down the mountain to the creek bottom. The snow was seven or eight feet deep and I fell through a snow bridge, getting both feet wet. It was below zero and a long way to timber whichever way I turned, a little nearer turning back, but I never like hitting the back trail. It was eight o'clock at night before I crossed the summit of the pass and reached the first timber. I got a fire started, but it was drifting and snowing so hard that the snow covered my sox and moccasins as fast as I could wring them dry, and, owing to the fierce wind, the flames leaped in every direction, making it impossible to get near the fire, so at half past nine I gave it up, put on my wet footgear and snowshoes and started down the valley. I could not see and felt the way with a stick. By daylight I had made three and a half miles; not much, but it kept the circulation going. In the heavy timber I made a fire and got dried out. My feet were beginning to pain as they had been thawed out twice already. I made three miles more that day and finished the last of my grub. The big snowshoes sank fifteen inches in the soft new snow and were a heavy drag on frozen toes. I saw it meant three or four more days tramping without grub to make Laggan. I made it in three, but the last day I could only make about fifty yards without resting, and my back tracks did not leave a very straight line. The chief trouble I had was to keep from

Cyril and George Paris, 1909; George Paris.

that fierce pain would drive away sleep; that he had no food, and always before him those interminable, slow, dragging miles of snowy wilderness. It must have required iron determination to make the end of that neverending track, to eat his Christmas dinner with his wife and family.

Even such an awful experience could not dull Tom's keen native wit, and his remark to the doctor while examining his poor feet, "I hope I won't have to lose them, Doctor, I've had 'em a long time and I'm sort of used to 'em," shows the spirit of the man. We are happy to add that Mr. Wilson is now progressing well towards recovery. He has lost part of several toes on each foot, but as he says himself, the doctor has left him well balanced, by taking the same number of toes from each foot, and he can't complain.

going to sleep; it would have been so much easier to quit than to go on."

Mr. Wilson concludes his letter with the remark, "I think this is the longest letter I ever wrote."

Think for a moment what it really meant; that every time he put on his snowshoes his toes got frozen owing to the tight shoe straps; that every time he took them off his feet had to be thawed out; that every step had to raise a load of ten to fifteen pounds of soft snow; that wood had to be collected and cut to keep alive during the night;

Banff in Storm King's Grip

Sunday's Storm most Severe in Twenty Years...Reminiscences of 1896

Crag, Jan. 29, 1916

For the past several days Banff has been in the grip of the storm king and although there has been no actual suffering, many people have been greatly inconvenienced by frozen water pipes and zero weather in their homes.

Snow started to fall last Friday afternoon and continued without intermission until Sunday afternoon when it culminated in a miniature blizzard. Some 26 inches of snow fell on the level, and the gale of Sunday piled the snow in drifts rendering navigation of the streets almost impossible. The mercury dropped rapidly, reaching the extreme low point of 46.5 below zero during the Sunday night.

"Gentleman George grabbed the women and children and threw them into the deep snow..."

All the trains from the west were cancelled owing to trouble in the mountains. The first eastbound train to arrive in Banff for a period of 48 hours reached here Tuesday afternoon and it was made up at Revelstoke.

The extreme cold, ranging from 30 to 40 below zero, in addition to the cutting wind kept citizens confined to their homes, no one venturing to leave the shelter of their fireside unless absolutely compelled to do so.

This was the most severe storm experienced in Banff in twenty years.

On Nov. 17, 1896, there was a snow fall beside which the present one was but an infant. The storm lasted for 48 hours, beginning at 5 o'clock Friday afternoon and continuing until 7 p.m. the following Sunday, during which five feet of snow fell on the level and the mercury dropped to 40 below the zero mark.

Old-timers retain a vivid recollection of this, also of how Hector Crawler and Gentleman George, his brother, lost a band of fine horses and narrowly escaped losing their lives as well. The two chiefs of the Stony tribe of Indians had come over from the Kootenay with their wives and papooses and a string of choice race horses. They had got as far as Mount Edith pass when overtaken by the storm and were advised to make the balance of the trip over the C.P.R. right-of-way. Against the better judgement of Chief Hector they started along the railway track when a light engine crashed into the band. Gentleman George grabbed the women and children and threw them into the deep snow along the track, but the horses were cut to pieces and Chief Crawler struck by the engine and severely injured. Hector was one of the wealthiest Indians of his tribe but his entire capi-

Ice boat fishing on Devil's Lake (Lake Minnewanka), circa 1890; *S.A. Smyth.*

tal was invested in his string of race horses and their loss practically broke him. He was a mad Indian and vowed to shoot the engineer on sight, a vow he would undoubtedly have kept had not the railway men deemed it prudent to seek a change of climate.

Robert E. Campbell, I Would Do It Again, 1959

Elliott Barnes was a Minnesotan who had started a horse ranch on Kootenay Plains but who wintered in Banff. He was also the possessor of a camera that could be speeded up to one-twelve hundredths of a second. Having never seen ice-boats in action, he was desirous of getting some snaps. Then came a Sunday that filled the bill, clear weather and very strong wind.

The show was to take place down the lake between Gibraltar and Mount Aylmer. There the ice was not only clear, but the lake at its widest. The boats were all lined up for a photo ensemble. Then a number of us got on Captain Jack's Windjammer for the sail by. Jack got his boat down to its slowest and we all stood up for the picture. Barnes was sure he had caught it. Now Jack came up with a stunt performance. He would upset the boat and our camera man would snap it in the act of going over. To add to the show, would someone stand on it while it was being upset? I volunteered. We would go

Barnes family boating on Willow Creek, 1907; *Elliott Barnes*

back across the lake and make the run down on the wind-ward side of the photographer. I was to stand on the starboard beam-side, clutching the mainstay. The mast would prevent the boat from going all the way over, and the shot would be made while I was hanging from the stay. Jack manipulated the boat perfectly. Swinging it broadside to the wind, over it went. To make certain success, would we do it again? Sure! So off we went across the lake for a second performance. We had come about half way across when…

When I regained consciousness a couple of days later Dr. Harry Brett asked me if I remembered what had happened. I thought I remembered someone placing a cigarette in my mouth. He smiled. No, it wasn't a cigarette. Driving through Bankhead he had stopped at Dr. Taylor's and given me a dose of strychnine. Why that? To keep my heart pumping.

Lake Minnewanka

Crag, 1907

The translation from the Indian "Water Spirits," is one of the many beautiful spots around Banff and even more so is the drive to reach this place.

Many are the old Indian legends told of these waters: of how the lake is supposed to be inhabited by a wonderful and hideous spirit, which takes great offence at any noise pertaining to singing. This was demonstrated one day, for while a canoe full of Indian

Lois and Oscar Barnes, circa 1906; *Elliott Barnes.*

women and children were fishing for the trout that abound in these waters, they thoughtlessly commenced a chant. Suddenly out of the water appeared the huge back of a fish many yards broad, only to disappear when out shot a beautifully shaped arm and hand, which clutched not in vain at one of the singers. Immediately a companion seized a knife and stabbed the arm through and through. The hand only clung the tighter to its victim and the surrounding waters were churned and lashed about as if the winds of heaven were let loose all at once. The canoe was finally capsized and only one of the party got to shore to tell the story.

A Pleasant Fishing Party

Crag, June 7, 1902

A very happy trio of fishermen in the shape of three ambassadors of commerce from Winnipeg, pulled off from W. Mather's boat house last Monday morning. Following the stream up into a narrow entrance of Vermilion lake, here the three sportsmen threw in their lines for unsuspecting trout. The game went merrily on until Mr. Carmichael suddenly got a nibble as the float on his line told. The nibble turned into a good strong tug which told in silent words the rest of the party that the lucky fisherman had Mr. Trout hooked. Now, Mr. Carmichael never told the rest of the party that this trip was his debut in the finny circles, though intimately acquainted with fishing tackle of all descriptions. On Mr. Carmichael getting the fish well hooked, or the fish getting himself hooked, he let a yell out of him that would have done credit to a red man of 1885, and with a tremendous pull the trout was landed, not on the bank or in the boat, but into the lap of a lady belonging to another party who were fishing beside him.

The lady proved herself a fisherman, for quietly unhooking the trout she dropped him into her own basket with a thank you.

Crag, July 15, 1922

A lady guest at the Banff Springs hotel was fishing in the Spray river last week and while throwing the line over her shoulder to make a cast she hooked a gopher. The rodent was firmly attached to the fish hook, but the fair disciple of Isaac Walton killed it with a bottle. Our informant did not state whether the bottle was empty or otherwise.

A Remarkable Occurrence

Crag, April 1, 1901

F. Beattie's cow, while crossing the river near Mather's boat house last Thursday, broke through the ice and came near losing her life. When rescued from her icy bath, a good sized trout was discovered wriggling in one of her forehoofs.

Circa 1890; *Boorne and May.*

(1032.) BIG FISH, FROM DEVIL'S LAKE, BANFF.
B.9667

Elliott Barnes, Kootenay Plains, 1907; *Elliott Barnes.*

James Simpson's letters to Dr. J. Monroe Thorington, AAJ, 1976

In September 1904, I left to go trapping up the Alexandra River and parts north. Visiting Kootenay Plains to get my horses I promised Tom Wilson to visit him on Christmas. Five days before that festive day I am seventy miles north, so for five days I snowshoed south and I had a lot of fur and I wanted to keep wolverine from breaking into my cabin and destroying it in my absence. So I packed up some grub and knew I could make it and arrived at his trader's cabin on Xmas Eve. He was so pleased to see me that we got gloriously tight on Hudson's Bay rum until daylight. On Christmas day he was a little moody and next noon he says "When in Hell are you going back?" So I left at noon, taking two of my horses and camped seven miles west for the night in heavy rain. Next morning I found my horses had swum the Saskatchewan River with hobbles on, so I put everything on my back, told them what I thought of them and started northwest for the Alexandra River on foot. Up the North Saskatchewan I nearly had serious trouble. It had snowed an inch in my absence and when I stepped on the ice the water had backed up, then froze and the ice cracked under me just above a thirty-foot waterfall and my snowshoes, still on my feet, were in the water, I could not kick them off and

Rudolph Aemmer and Paul Konig, 1912.

for fur or rather marten tracks somewhere. The marten who were making the tracks never materialized.

I went back up the Alexandra River and finished the winter in and about Thompson Pass. That was where on a beautiful night I heard orchestration coming from Mt. Lyell, from the southwest and passing over me and fading away to the northeast, travelling in an arc, and me following it right overhead until it faded away. I was not dreaming or just bushed, but it was very real. I could hear the violins most clearly, no drums or other instruments, and I knew not what the air was, but it was beautiful. I do not talk about it often as I know people think it incredible or a bad dream; but not so, I was on my feet, wide awake and mystified. It happened long before there was radio.

they were the only pair I had with me, but having my heavy mackinaw pants on which were rough I stuck to the ice and finally got my fingers into a crack above me and managed to pull myself out, much wiser than before. Having a pole and brush teepee under a concave rock quite handy I put in the night there quite comfortable.

Tom was not trapping. He could not trap a mouse if it was eating off the same breakfast plate as he was, but he was trading foodstuffs with the Indians

Hunting Parties Get Some Fine Game Specimens

Crag, Sept. 29, 1917

Two of New York's most noted men, Dr. A.G. Bugbee, and Carl Run-

gius, the noted painter, returned on Monday from travelling over the mountains in search of game and subjects for paintings, and both are not only satisfied with their trips and the results obtained, but are so enthusiastic over the country travelled, that they "set up" one of the swellest meals ever laid down in Banff hotels, to the guides and packers who accompanied him, at the Mount Royal hotel on Tuesday night.

"The big game hunters knelt and began filling the mountain side with lead."

Dr. Bugbee, who is a New York specialist, was accompanied by his wife, and four weeks ago, with Jimmy Simpson, the noted guide and outfitter, as guide, Jack Powell as cook, and H. Deegan as horse wrangler and assistant, the party set out for the head waters of the North Saskatchewan and Cataract rivers on a hunting trip. There they found game plentiful, and secured some splendid trophies, which the doctor packed away in his trunks and took to New York with him as souvenirs of the best and most exciting trip he ever made into the wilds on a hunting trip. The doctor who has travelled in many different parts of the States in search of game and other forms of recreation, is loud in his praises of this country, and has decided to tell all the people of New York to get out in the country around Banff for splendid game. He left for home on Wednesday night.

Carl Rungius, with a different outfit, Jimmy Boyce and Mac. Brooks, covered practically the same ground, only going by a different route, and his success was no less than that of Dr. Bugbee. He also got all the law allows, and in addition got renewed inspiration for the famous painting he is working on, "The Trail," a painting of a pack train on Wilcox Pass, north of Lake Louise. During his absence Mr. Rungius received an invitation from the Chicago Art Institute to exhibit this picture at its thirtieth annual exhibition, at which only fifty paintings are accepted. This is considered a distinctive recognition of Mr. Rungius' ability. It is generally accepted that the paintings by this artist of the scenery and animals in Western Canada, is among the best advertising this country gets.

Helen Breeze Walcott, Mount Assiniboine, circa 1925; *Byron Harmon.*

Letter from Rev. George Kinney to Dr. J. Monroe Thorington, 1934

In our party were two fine fellows from the city of Washington, Dr. Walcott's son was one. These two youths were our "Big game hunters" for trophies for the Smithsonian Institute. They were good hunters but unlucky, and Conrad and Curlie Phillips would on occasion go out a little and shoo in a flock of goats or sheep or a few caribou in order that our specialists of the Institution might have something of size to stuff. We were in camp near Berg Lake. Our climbers were having a day off from strenuous work, and had been busy here and there, when Harmon, who had been up the Robson glacier after pictures, came rushing into camp wildly shouting "bear, bear." Out tumbled the "Big Game" hunters wildly scrambling after Harmon, the guide. Conrad and Curlie seized what weapons were handy, and I trailed behind efficiently armed with two ten-inch twenty tews. We were making a comedy of what was a serious matter for the hunters.

At last we discovered the black bear on the mountain side above us. The big game hunters knelt and began filling the mountain side with lead. Their magazines were soon emptied and Conrad and I each got behind one of the hunters and pulled the shells out of their belts and handed them the ammunition as needed during the terrific bombardment.

The bear, in the meantime dodged here and there or else watched curiously what was going on. He was finally hit by a stray shot and scuried (sic) out of sight.

In 1916 John Singer Sargent, the Eminent Society Painter Visited the Rockies

August 20,

I am camping under that waterfall that Mr. Denman Ross gave me a postcard of. It is magnificent when the sun shines which it did for the first two days. I began a picture—that is ten days ago—and since then it has been raining and snowing steadily—provisions and temper getting low—but I shall stick it out till the sun reappears. Tell Mr. Ross that he was quite right, but that now there is only one fall of the "Twins," thanks to some landslip above ... Your handerkerchiefs are in constant use and still hold out in spite of a dripping nose & cold feet.

August 28

Camping out near Mount Stephen House, Field, British Columbia.

I am about to move on with my tents to some other valley within the reach of Field—two things have got on my nerves—one the roar and hissing and pounding all night long of a tremendous waterfall that I am near, the other the alighting of snowflakes

Hughie Sibbald, Dr. Harry Brett, Mary Sibbald, Red Deer River, 1913.

on my bottom when it is bared once a day. Perhaps this is the poetry of camping out.

August 30,

Dear Cousin Mary,

At the risk of importuning you with this persistent letter writing, here I go again. As I told you in my first or my last it was raining and snowing, my tent flooded, mushrooms sprouting in my boots, porcupines taking shelter in my clothes, canned food always fried in a black frying pan getting on my nerves, and a fine waterfall which was the attraction to the place pounding and thundering all night. I stood it for three weeks and yesterday came away with a repulsive picture. Now the weather has changed for the better and I am off again to try the simple life (ach pfui) in tents at the top of another valley, this time with a gridiron instead of a frying pan and a perforated India rubber mat to stand on. It takes time to learn how to be really happy.

Please take your courage in both hands and write me a line to this hotel. I will pounce upon it when I get back from my next plunge into canned food—thirty miles away.

F.N. Waterman, CAJ, 1923

That night, just as we were beginning to dream of path finding on the following day, we were aroused by a distant humming, very human in quality, proceeding from the direction of the tent occupied by Rudolph and Reno. It was repeated many times, at about thirty-second intervals, until the writer found himself humming in unison and wondering if Reno, the musician of the party, was practising in his sleep. The notes comprised a minor seventh and were rendered quite accurately in a seemingly inquiring mood. They are closely represented by the following:

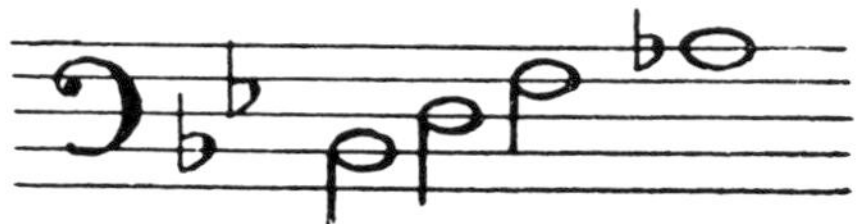

Presently there was a silence of a minute or two and then another phrase was sounded and repeated at shorter intervals:

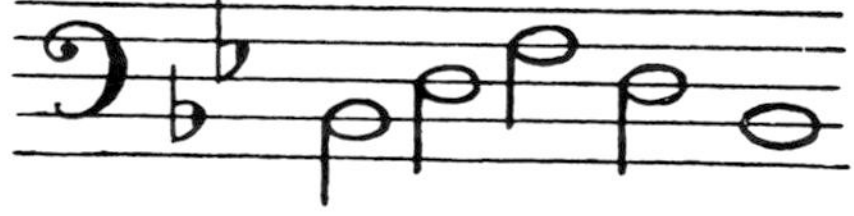

This one abandoned the minor interval and was sounded in a tone of supreme contentment. Presently the sound became louder and seemed to be moving towards us as though the singer, having finished his serenade at the other tent, was coming to honour us. When, however it came to rest at the saddle cache near the corner of our tent, the suspicion was aroused that the owner of the voice was not actuated by solely romantic impulses, and our flashlight revealed a rather diminutive porcupine industriously trying to work off the weighted cover, which Reno had thoughtfully placed over the saddles. Stockinged feet and a balky light, which went out just at the critical moment, combined to spare the tuneful singer for the entertainment of future campers, but he received punishment enough to cause him to remain at a respectable distance from our camp hereafter. The plentiful sprinklings of quills which marked his retreat indicated that pursuit would have been hazardous under the circumstances.

AT LAKE LOUISE

Crag, August 23, 1918

Nobody ever gets accustomed to Lake Louise. You come down in the morning, thinking of canteloupe and coffee. And at the stairhead you have your first—yes, it is a smashing glimpse of the lake.

"You can't paint it," declared Mr. Wilcox this year out of twenty-seven seasons' knowledge of its dancing moodiness. "You get your clouds and your rock colours in. Then you try for the water. But the clouds you painted are gone and this lake is quite different in tone from the lake that went with your light effect. You might work for years and never see the precise combination repeated that you tried to get—and got a maddening half of."

Mr. Wilcox made his second visit with some college friends in 1893 and this time he brought a camera, a little 5" by 7", that laid the foundation for all his future reputation in the world of

Lake O'Hara, circa 1909; *Walter D. Wilcox.*

psychological moment that brought the light I wanted on the water and the mountains."

Another scene the picture-maker coveted was the sparkling Giant's Steps in Paradise Valley.

"I worked on that falls for two days and I had a man to help me. We cut down a tree that interfered with the camera and we tidied up heaven knows how much rubbish. I don't believe in making a scene artificial but I do believe in making it artistically natural."

"The beginner doesn't get one plate in twelve," said Mr. Wilcox. "Often he spoils his whole dozen. You can be 'a little careless' and still have some sort of result in ordinary photography. But in color work, it's all or nothing.

"Nowadays I'm going over all the old beauty spots here in the new way. I have the composition worked out from my experiments of years ago. The precise location of the camera is marked in every case. All that I have to do is wait for the right light effect."

films and places.

In addition to the delicacy and correctness of his photographs, Mr. Wilcox can claim to have taken the largest picture ever achieved in Canada at a height of 10,000 feet. This is his panorama from Mt. Niblock with an 11" x 14" camera, and so real looking that a hot day makes you want to put it up beside the electric fan as a chill-producer.

Mr. Wilcox's famous Lake O'Hara study is another bit of wizardry.

"It took me just four years to get that one. I believe I brought the camera back at least ten times, and when I finally had a promising day, I waited from eight till twelve o'clock for the

Cora Johnstone Best, "Horse Thief Creek and the Lake of the Hanging Glaciers," CAJ, 1923

There hadn't been much said about it but those thirty-six sticks of dy-

Lake of the Hanging Glaciers, 1922; *Byron Harmon.*

namite had been carried all the way from Windermere on one of the horses (not Old Bill) to assist Nature in the final act of bringing forth a natural phenomenon. The act was to be called "The Birth of an Iceberg," in case it was an iceberg. Of course, the title could be changed in case it happened to be a monstrosity. It seems that when Freeman's party went up to the lake they had the same idea. Whether Harmon had purloined the act, after the Freeman failure, or whether the idea was common property I don't know, but I heard Harmon and Conrad discussing the possibilities. "Now" said Harmon, "you remember that when they touched off the dynamite, it made a lot of noise but that was all there was to it; there wasn't a chunk of ice big enough to photograph. And you remember that whale of an avalanche that came down from the jar of the explosion? It came right off that peak there and I'm going to focus on that same peak and I'm sure to get what they missed." Harmon wagged his head and we all stood around with satisfied smiles on our faces.

> *"He came down the stretch...his mane flying, his nostrils dilated and flaming, his eyes holding the fire of battle."*

The next morning broke just right. We were up early and in feverish haste to be off to the scene of action. Tom was sent for a horse and after a long while he came back with Old Bill, as he was the only one to be caught. The tripod, and camera boxes were loaded and we

Nello "Tex" Vernon-Wood and friend.

started for the lake. The exact spot for Harmon's moving picture camera had been picked out for days, also the exact spots for Mrs. Shippam's moving picture, and for each of their two still cameras. The whole scene had been gone over carefully so there would be nothing left undone that ought to be done.

Conrad went over and dug a hole in the ice and placed his dynamite, tamped it down and lighted the fuse. When he came back he remarked that something should come loose as there were seventeen sticks about to let go. Harmon took a last anxious look into the finder—yes, the exact peak, and it was rounded high with new snow. He mopped his face and looked along the lie to see if everything was ready. It was. This would be a grand success, undoubtedly. The earth shook; the air turned purple; Mother Earth agonized, and a few pounds of ice tinkled off into the water as the smoke drifted away. But, of course, that was understood. We were waiting for the aftermath, the mighty avalanche we were sure to get.

Now, when Old Bill had been unloaded he had strolled off to browse on some tufts of green and no one had given him a second thought. When the first report of the discharge took place, Old Bill started a little charge of his own. What mattered it to him if the cameras were in his line of advance? He came down the stretch hitting on all four, his mane flying, his nostrils dilated and flaming, his eyes holding the fire of battle. He hit Harmon first! Down went the camera and Old Bill walked up the spine of the vanquished photographer, hit the second, third and fourth cameras with sickening precision and careered off down the valley. And then it happened! The whole top of the mountain eased off a bit, toppled and crashed to the glacier below in the mightiest of the mighty of avalanches.

The most eloquently profane men never use words. This remark is not apropos of anyone in particular—I merely mention it as an observation of mine. After we had finished making out the casualty list, we collected our stuff and climbed, or rather scrambled, around the shore to the left of the lake where some fine pictures were procured by both Mrs. Shippam and Mr. Harmon.

TO A CAYUSE

B.W. Mitchell

Oh, patient Pinto of the tousled mane,
Standing all braced, your ears laid flatly back,
Your belly swelling as I take in slack
Of cinch rope, heaving taut with might and main
The diamond hitch—of pack-horse life the bane—
That aims to make of you and of your pack
One welded whole, as on steep trails you tack;
What thoughts run riot in your cunning brain?
Your dreamy eye sees two close growing trees
To bolt between and scrape your load away;
You plan the chance of steep descents to seize
To shiver loose your pack, whereby you may
Spread broadcast flour, cheese, bacon, blankets, tents,
Unheeding packers' lurid compliments.

A.A. McCoubrey, 1924; *Edward Feuz.*

MUSKEG

B.W. Mitchell

Obnoxious, pulpy, saturated mass,
Deluding reckless riders to their loss!
A plunging cayuse falls ere half across,
Mired in the toils of bottomless morass
Now deep in valleys, now on crest of pass,
The Pinto's down! Throw off the hitch and toss
His pack and mantle in the springy moss!
Entrapped! Poor Pinto sinks beneath the grass.
Muskeg! So innocent to untrained eyes;
Unhallowed bog to those who know you best.
Sweet flowers you flaunt whereon the butterflies,
Kin to the Fairies, flutter down to rest.
Exquisite orchids, lilies red as blood,
Green grasses, cover quivering depths of mud.

Wilf "My Little Old Yoho Lady" Carter, near Twin Falls Chalet, Yoho Valley, August 6, 1934; *"Tex" Wood.*

MOUNTAIN MONSTERS

A.C. Galt, "Consolidation Valley Annual Camp, 1910," CAJ, 1911

The ignorance of newcomers respecting the lingo of the mountains sometimes occasions embarrassment. As I sat smoking my pipe by the fire, a couple of Swiss guides were comparing notes on their preparatory examination of the mountains that afternoon, and were talking about Mt. Fay. Presently I caught the following remark: "It turned out to be not quite so large as I expected. Still, the forefoot extended down the valley about eighty yards and the snout was about fifteen feet." "Heavens alive!" thought I, "what kind of monster can this be, of such prodigious size?" I knew that there were some celebrated fossil beds near Mt. Stephen but I had no idea that monsters of such size as the guides were talking about had ever existed in the world. Not wishing, of course, to appear too much surprised, I remarked to one of them, "What's that you were speaking of? A fossil?" The guide looked around at me with a rather dubious expression on his face, and said, "No fossil at all, solid ice." "Oh," said I to myself, "I have it now." I recalled the accounts of mammoths found away up in the Yukon and in Siberia, embedded in solid ice, where they must have lain entombed for perhaps thousands of years, and yet their bodies were preserved intact. But a monster of such gi-

ACC Annual Camp, Consolation Valley, 1910; *Byron Harmon.*

gantic size as above indicated was indeed a find. I determined to join the very first party scheduled for Mt. Fay, and hurried off to put down my name on the bulletin board.

Feeling very much interested in what promised to be one of the greatest discoveries of science, I rejoined my friends at the fire, and found by this time that the other guide was describing the situation on Mt. Bident. "What do you think of our chances tomorrow?" "Well," was the rejoinder, "I had a long pull around the left shoulder for several hours, with no very great difficulty until I got more than half-way up, when I caught sight of a bergschrund. It looked ugly. I would not care to face it alone, but possibly three or four of us with a rope might tackle it successfully."

I thought I was fairly well acquainted with the names of wild animals that might be expected in the mountains, but I had never before heard of this one, and had no desire to make his acquaintance. You see, the Government had prohibited the use of fire-arms throughout this part of the Rocky Mountains, and I felt that perhaps I might be a little in the way when the brute was being lassoed. But having put my name down for Mt. Fay, I hazarded the remark, "Any bergschrunds on Mt. Fay?" "Yes, indeed," said the guide, "a bigger and worse one than what I saw on Bident."

This was enough for me; I remembered my first determination not to try the mountains too hurriedly, so I con-

On Mount Richardson, ACC Annual Camp, Ptarmigan Valley, 1915.

cluded that I would wait until these horrible brutes had been successfully captured and brought into camp, before I would attempt either mountain. I therefore quietly slipped away and erased my name from the bulletin board, and turned in for the night, not altogether satisfied with the outlook.

Next morning at daybreak the President crept into the tent and roused the Rev. Mr. Wallace, who had put down his name for Mt. Bident. I must confess to having felt somewhat guilty in allowing an unsuspecting stranger to attempt a very dangerous task, but I remembered that my tent-mate was a contributor to "Rod and Gun", and thought he might resent my suggestions of inability to cope with big game.

After breakfast I concluded to take

the Secretary into my confidence, and found him busily engaged in the official tent. After I had outlined to him the incident with the guides the night before, he smiled quizzically, and taking up the first volume of the Alpine Club Journal, he turned to the glossary of mountain terms and said, "I think a perusal of a few pages of this will assist you in understanding the language of the guides." I hastily ran down the list of terms and their definitions, and having twice read over the definitions of "forefoot", "snout", and "bergschrund", I thanked the Secretary for his assistance, and requested that he would regard our interview as confidential.

"The Giants' Stairs," ACC Annual Camp, Paradise Valley, 1907; *Byron Harmon.*

WHO KILLED THE SHEEP?

Was it a Two-Legged or a Four-Legged Coyote? 'Tis a Burning Question

Crag, November 25, 1916

Monday a couple of game wardens, re-enforced by a member of the local detachment of the R.N.W.M.P., visited several homes and places of business in Banff and unceremoniously searched the premises. In the majority of instances care was taken to ascertain that the "man of the house" was absent before visiting premises.

It appears that some game warden, or other sleuth, while pussyfooting about in the hills came upon the carcase of a dead sheep and at once jumped to the conclusion that someone had shot the animal.

ODE TO THE MOSQUITO

B.C. 1887, J.A. Lee and W.J. Clutterbuck

A FRAGMENT

Recitative

On other poets here I place my veto,
Be mine alone to sing the dashed mosquito:

Aria

Thou airy sprite, child of the shady grove,
Faithful companion wheresoe'er we rove,
Together have we roamed the wide world through,
And thou alone of all its hosts art true.
On Afric's shores, on India's coral strand,
The first to meet us in this Northern land:
The last to leave us as its shores recede,
O ghostly gimlet, "treu and fest" indeed.
E'en as a watchful mother bends above
Her babe, and croons a lullaby of love,
So thou, whene'er our nightly couch we seek,
Hov'rest aloft, a "phantom—with a beak".
And with thy sweet small soul-entrancing song,
Thou'lt charm our wakeful ear the whole night long;
When pain and anguish chance to wring the brow.
No wife so constant at our side as thou.
But unlike woman, in our hours of ease,
Thou'rt not uncertain, coy, or hard to please;
Content to dwell upon the merest speck
Of ear or nose, or small expanse of neck.

Yet some repay with base ingratitude
The unending toil of all thy winged brood
Into vile durance some would gladly cram
Both "all thy pretty chickens and their dam"

And some anticipate with joy the day
When autumn chill and drear cuts short thy stay
Ah me! too soon that day must come at last,
And thou must die 'neath winter's icy blast

Too soon — for still thy birthplace and thy doom
Are hid in nature's deep mysterious gloom.
Com'st thou from heaven? Nay, we cannot tell,
Nor whither wending, but we hope, to

Acting upon this deduction, and without the formality of securing a search warrant, they promptly made a raid upon the homes of citizens whom they, in their wisdom, suspected of being poachers or of having wild mutton in their possession illegally.

The search was not productive of results, no quarters of mutton being found that could by the wildest stretch of the imagination be made to fit upon the carcase of the deceased sheep.

The searchers are looking very wise and vaguely hinting that they have a card up their sleeves, but the owners of the premises searched are not worrying—simply waiting for a show down.

> "...care was taken to ascertain that the "man of the house" was absent."

While not upholding law-breakers in the Canadian National Park, nor endorsing their acts in any shape or form, this paper voices the sentiment of the Park population when it asserts that the wholesale searching of private houses and hotels by game wardens and the R.N.W.M.P., without a search warrant duly signed by the proper authority, is un-British in every sense of the word. It is safe to add that there are houses in Banff where, had the men folks been at home, this unseemly searching would not have taken place—despite the wording of the Game Act. Thousands of men are laying down their lives today in Europe for the upholding of the very principles which the Banff game wardens are endeavoring to trample under foot.

PAID FANCY PRICE FOR MUTTON

James Simpson convicted of Shooting Rocky Mountain Sheep within Park limits

Crag, December 9, 1916

The police court room was crowded Wednesday afternoon with citizens anxious to hear the trial of James Simpson, charged with killing mountain sheep within Park limits.

The accused was charged by H.E. Sibbald, chief game guardian, with three separate and distinct offenses, as follows: With killing a mountain sheep three and a-half miles west of Banff, along the motor road, on or about Nov. 18; with unlawfully having portions of a mountain sheep in his possession; with having killed a mountain sheep near the 7 mile post on the motor road on or about Nov. 14. Defendant pleaded not guilty to all three accounts.

J.R. Warren, game guardian, deposed to having followed fresh buggy tracks along the motor road on the morning of Nov. 19, the rig had turned around 3 1/2 miles west of town, saw

Sidney Vick, Superintendent Jack Clarke, and Jock Stewart (Jock-the-noo) with the ram the Banff Museum eventually sent to Jasper as an example of a badly mounted specimen, circa 1920.

spots of blood on the snow, traced the tracks back as far as the railway crossing where they were lost, went back up the road in the afternoon with Sibbald and Peyto, searched the vicinity and found carcase of a dead sheep hidden under a pile of logs, discovered the head 25 yards away under another log pile, the scalp and four legs of the animal were missing, cleaned the carcase and found that the animal had been shot through the heart.

Game Guardians W.G. Fyfe and C. Philips testified to having been present when the scalp seized at Simpson's residence was fitted to the carcase, every notch in the skin fitted perfectly.

H.E. Sibbald, J.R. Warren and W.H. Peyto testified that on the following Monday, Nov. 20, they, in company with Corporal Baker, searched Simpson's residence, and found the scalp of a sheep and a quantity of wild game meat in the attic.

The foregoing witnesses were severally cross-examined by Mr. Simpson.

Bert Sibbald, U. LaCasse, Hugh Gordon and Wm. Warren were called and testified for the defense. Their evidence was mainly of a nature calculated to prove that the scalp did not belong to the carcase, that the meat was not sheep meat and that Simpson was in their company or seen by them on the dates the animal was supposed to have been shot.

The third case was then called. C. Phillips, game guardian, testified to having found tracks of a man in the bush along the motor road near the 7 mile post on Nov. 14, later found the carcase of a dead sheep which had been shot and rolled down the mountain side.

Art. Bryant, of the 15th Light Horse, testified to having met Simpson near the 7 mile post on the afternoon of Nov. 14.

Simpson cross-examined the witnesses and took the stand in his own defense.

The court found Simpson guilty in each of the three counts. As it was his first conviction, the judge imposed the minimum fines — $50 and costs for the first and $25 and costs each for the second and third offenses. The total amounted to $126.00, which was paid forth-with.

Credit is due to the game guardians for the manner in which they worked up the cases, establishing a strong chain of circumstantial and direct evidence.

Norman Luxton, circa 1910; *George Paris.*

(Crag, November 7, 1914)

"Banff," the big moose, is chumming with the men on the water extension ditch, eating portions of their lunch and drinking from their water pails. It is said the other moose have ostracized "Banff" on account of his 20 cents an hour predilection.

Crag, May 14, 1906

Sing a song of wildcat, raise a little scare, one on Tunnel Mountain, William saw it there. Four boys hunted pussy, Thursday of this week, but they couldn't find her, and she's still to seek.

PREHISTORIC LIZARD FOUND AT EXSHAW

Crag, June 7, 1913

At the Exshaw Cement Mines last week, while cracking open a huge block of rock, a prehistoric lizard about 6 inches long was found in the centre of the rock encased completely by the rocky formation where it had apparently been hermetically sealed for thousands of years. The lizard was

Lorne Orr, Jim Brewster and grizzly skin, circa 1930; *Byron Harmon.*

freed from its prison and placed in the sunlight where it remained motionless for about an hour, when it drew several long breaths and slowly opened its bright eyes, it then assumed a ruddy color. The finder thinking it needed a stimulant put a few drops of brandy down its throat, and the lizard then became quite lively, raised on its hind leg, and fell dead. It is now preserved in Alcohol. These finds are very unusual.

KILLED BY GRIZZLY

A Young Swede Laborer Meets Death near the Spray Lakes

Crag, October 10, 1914

Oscar Lovgren, a young Swede, was killed by a grizzly Monday afternoon near the Spray Lakes.

The news reached town Monday evening and Howard Sibbald left for the scene of the killing Tuesday. The body was recovered and brought to Canmore, where Coroner Thomson held an inquest Wednesday.

The facts brought out at the inquest are as follows: Lovgren, who was only

24 years of age had been in Canada for about twelve months, was at the lumber camp near the Spray lakes with a companion named Wilson waiting to be put to work, although not on the pay roll. Monday Lovgren took a rifle, belonging to Gombart one of the foremen, and went out to look for a bear that had been reported as being in the neighborhood of the camp. He returned to the camp at noon and reported having found the bear and killed it, firing five bullets into Bruin. After eating dinner he, with two companions, went out to skin the bear and bring in the meat. When they arrived at the spot where he had "killed" the animal the bear was not there, but a trail of blood disclosed its whereabouts and the three hunters confidently approached the wounded beast without using precautions to ascertain if it were really and truly dead.

Tying a bear to the bars at the Banff Zoo, circa 1925.

Lovgren, who was still carrying the rifle, was slightly in the rear of his two companions when with a blood-curdling roar the wounded grizzly rose to her feet and, ignoring the two men in front, made straight for the man with the gun. Lovgren had no time to shoot and with one sweep of her mighty paw the man's face was torn off and his skull crushed to a jelly. The other two men lost no time in making their get-away and, reaching camp, gave the alarm.

When Sibbald arrived at the scene of the killing, which is reached by pack trail through White Man's Pass, he

Mrs. Scarth with Monty and Kathleen and Norman Luxton's bear, circa 1907; *George Paris.*

found the bear, a female grizzly, stone dead about 200 yards from where Lovgren had been killed. The carcase contained five bullets.

A coroner's jury, composed of S. Stirton, foreman, A.B. Latimer, F.W. Knott, C. Diamond, A.E. Grainger and T. Lowden, was empanelled. After hearing the evidence, substantially as above, the jury returned with a verdict of accidental death.

> *"...the man's face was torn off and his skull crushed to a jelly."*

Serg't Oliver, of the R.N.W.M.P. Canmore, laid an information against Gombart for having in his possession an unsealed rifle within limits of the Rocky Mountain Park, and F.W. Knott, J.P., disposed of the case by imposing a fine of $25.00 and costs.

Beware of Wild Animals

Crag, August 14, 1925

The Calgary Albertan published an article this morning which to our mind is very detrimental to the tourist trade, under the caption, "Winter will be early, severe, by actions of Rocky animals," displaying same on the front page. Whether or not the item has been published as a joke is beyond our comprehension, but in our opinion—it is certainly misleading. It should be the policy of the Calgary papers to boost our National Park, and not to publish such articles as appeared in the morning paper to-day, which will tend to keep tourists away from the little mountain resort. Two paragraphs of the article are reproduced herewith:

Curly Phillips' bear cub with J.W. Beatty, RCA, 1914; *P.L.Tait.*

"An early severe winter is forecast this year by the unusual actions of the wild animals in the Rocky Mountains. *The most untamable man-fearing beasts* have already come down from the heights of their summer abode and have become so tame that they are being fed from the human hand in the back yards of Banff homes. Bear, elk, and antelope are *literally walking the streets of Banff in broad daylight with no show of fear in their demeanor.*

"Not until this week has there ever been any record here of the *ferocious cinnamon bear fraternizing with human beings.* But since last Monday a large yellow specimen of this man-hating bear has been calling daily at the back door of Sir James Lougheed's home, begging for food, standing on his hind legs."

NOTE—The Italics are the Editor's.

Crag, June 21, 1919

A young lady visitor, while inspecting the zoo Sunday, was overheard to remark: "She wished she was a beaver." She was leaning over the basin in which a lone beaver was disporting over a shoal of trout at the time, and the poor worm of a man with her instead of leading the way to a café and a fish dinner said, "Let's go watch the polar bear wag his fool head." No wedding bells for him! The poetry of romance and scenery is wasted on such a lout.

> *"The most untamable man-fearing beasts have already come down from the heights..."*

DEAD! YET ALIVE!

Crag, June 28, 1913

The Park Government recently bought four Albino Gophers from Brooks, Alberta. For several weeks they were busy in the old pheasant hut, digging holes and answering the thousand questions the wandering public asked.

Two of the gophers tired of the job and to all intent and purpose died. One was sure dead, for customery of these animals he had been partly eaten by his white brothers. Mr. Sanson, curator of the Museum, took the dead ones to the Sign of the Goat Curio Store, to be mounted last Tuesday morning. Charley Prior, Taxidermist, prepared his table for the skinning of the dead, but was called away for a couple of hours and on his return discovered the gopher that was not partly eaten had moved to the opposite side of the table where he had left it. Amazed, he picked the gopher up and commenced artificial respiration with an occasional drop of spirits and water, with the results that after he had been dead 36 hours he came to life and ate a hearty meal of greens. Again the next morning the gopher was dead and after 60 hours he was once more brought to life, with the assistance of an electric light globe to heat the box in which he was kept. He was kept alive for four days, only dying twice. At the end of the fifth day he died, and Charley tired of his life saving stunt skinned him and "deaded" him for sure. The pair of these gophers can be seen at the Curio Store for the next ten days, when they will be returned to the Government Museum.

Crag, July 30, 1921

Lewis Mumford, game warden at Johnston Canyon, is spending a portion of his spare hours in gentling a young black bear and the taming process has proceeding sufficiently that Bruin will eat food out of his hand.

It is rumored that when the taming is completed the Super will commandeer the bear and either place him in the Cave or teach him to wash windows at the government bath-house.

Sunday drive to Lake Minnewanka, circa 1915; *Byron Harmon.*

Banff News, May 31, 1930

Death called one of Banff's most beautiful visitors Saturday. For the past three weeks a bear and two tiny cubs have endeared themselves to visitors to the resort. The little animals learned to climb on the running boards of automobiles and beg for tidbits.

Saturday one of the cubs jumped off a running board in the path of an approaching automobile and was killed. The mother bear enraged pursued the automobile for a distance and then returned to her cub. She nuzzled the lifeless body, voicing sad cries. A fascinated crowd saw the bereaved mother sadly pick up the bruised little body and carry it away into the bush far from curious eyes.

AUTOMOBILES TO RUN IN BANFF

Next Season, Which Means that the Horse Must Go as the Trails are Too Dangerous for Both

Crag, October 24, 1914

The summer of 1915 will, in all probability, see automobiles running in the Rocky Mountains Park and on every street and road in Banff, with the single exception of the trail leading to the Upper Hot Springs, if the proposed amendments and extensions to the regulations governing the use of motor vehicles in the Park, by the Commissioner of Dominion Parks, receive the stamp of approval by Order in Council.

George Fowles and Ted Davidson, circa 1916; Dan McCowan.

Crag, June 15, 1912

New buildings, new sign boards and a most remarkable increase of tourists and visitors have convinced even the most hard-shelled moss-back in Banff that a new era has arrived and Banff has discarded its swaddling clothes and is beginning to take steps—more or less uncertain, as is natural for its tender age—towards the future.

We get the Calgary tinhorn sport arrayed, like Solomon, in a pair of multi-shaded tan shoes with toes that look like they were infected with a case of double mumps, a bow tie which in its effulgence looks like whiskers on a Thomas cat. This creature is so enamoured of itself that it speaks to every unescorted woman, displaying a Jack Johnsonian grin that not only demonstrates its owner's atrophied cerebral convolutions but also his crying need of even the roughest kind of a dentist.

Then we have the pseudo man-about-town dressed in a pair of peg top trousers—three axe handles across and a carrying capacity of about six sacks of salt—a chorus girl overcoat and a Swiss "yodelling" hat that is made in "Keebeck". This missing link perches on the railings of the bridge, much as his antedeluvian ancestors used to hang by their tails to primeval trees, and like them chatter blatantly at and for the benefit of passing women, filling the air with would-be funny remarks and the odour of a bad breath and a third rate rye.

Crag, June 1, 1912

Among the Calgarians who came up on last night's crowded train for the weekend were G.M. Lang, Miss Lang and maid; Dr. M.G. McRae, of the Western Canada College; Stanley L. Jones; Mr. and Mrs. Fred Lowes and party; and many others. A large number of motor cars are coming up today, and the owners of the first car in, who made the trip in less than five hours, say the road is in excellent condition.

A quick dip in a cold mountain stream, circa 1925; *Caroline Hinman.*

SALE OF LOTS

In the Townsite of Banff Realizes $1,623

Crag, May 23, 1914

The auction sale of cancelled and vacant lots in the townsite of Banff, held at the government office last Saturday, resulted in the disposal of 54 lots, at prices ranging from $2.00 to $250.00. The highest price was paid for lot 15 in block 4 by W.G. Richardson, after spirited bidding. The total receipts of the sale amounted to $1,623.00.

Col. Maynard Rodgers, superintendent of Jasper Park, was the auctioneer and considerable of the success of the sale should be credited to that gentleman's urbanity and courteous demeanor. As one purchaser remarked, "The colonel could sell gold bricks, were he so inclined."

A busy day in Banff, circa 1915. The bridge was moved downstream a few feet in 1914 to prepare for the new bridge which was finished in 1923. *Whyte Collection.*

Crag, June 17,1911

Senator Forget and Mrs. Forget are in the old Bell-Irving house on Beaver avenue, while the Senator is having his lot at the corner of Buffalo and Muskrat cleared to build a summer bungalow. This section of Banff promises to be the finest built in the entire townsite. The view from the Senator's lots is magnificent and it is no wonder that these properties along Buffalo avenue have advanced in value from a few dollars to $1,000-each. The Senator intends making Banff his summer home and Ottawa his winter residence. The hon. gentleman is a big addition to Banff residents, and with an ex-Governor, a premier, three senators, some judges, more lawyers and a sheriff, Banff should in time get what the people want from Ottawa.

Treasure Trove on Whiskey Creek

Barrel of Moonshine Whiskey said to have been Buried Thirty Years Ago

Crag, June 24, 1916

For more than a quarter of a century the story has been kept rife by that elusive jade, Dame Rumor, that treasure trove awaited the successful seeker along the banks of Whiskey creek. And many a Banffite, who ordinarily would look with eyes of scorn upon the plebian pickaxe and spade, has armed himself with those implements of husbandry and, under the moon's wan silvery light, toiled manfully and long in quest of the buried treasure. But success has not, so far, crowned the efforts of the spasmodic searchers.

The treasure is not gold, neither is it composed of silver or precious stones. But, now that Alberta is going "dry" the first of July, it is something of far more inestimable value in the eyes of many men. It can best be described by borrowing the following from the pen of that silver-tongued orator and past-master of the king's English—the late Colonel Robert G. Ingersoll:

"Drink it, and you will hear the voices of men and maidens singing the 'Harvest Home,' mingled with the laughter of children."

"It is some of the most wonderful whiskey that ever drove the skeleton from a feast or painted landscapes in the brain of man. It is the mingled souls of wheat and corn. In it you will find the sunshine and the shadow that chased each other over the billowy fields, the breath of June, the carol of the lark, the dews of night, the wealth of summer and the autumn's rich content—all golden with imprisoned light. Drink it, and you will hear the voices of men and maidens singing the 'Harvest Home,' mingled with the laughter of children. Drink it, and you will feel within your blood the star-lit dawn, the dreamy tawny dusk of many perfect days. For thirty years this liquid joy has been within the happy staves of oak, longing to touch the lips of man."

Some thirty odd years ago, long before Alberta had arisen to the dignity of a province, prohibition was popularly supposed to be rigidly enforced in the Northwest Territories. It was possible, however, for a man with a thirst to secure a permit which entitled him to ship in a certain amount of liquid refreshments. Illicit purveyors of the "forbidden fruit" were plentiful in those days—as they undoubtedly will be after July 1st—and one of the favorite methods of bringing the booze into Banff in the early 80's, while the C.P.R. construction work was under way, was to unload the pack ponies at the foot of Cascade mountain and cache the casks along the bed of the creek—hence the name Whiskey Creek.

Later on, soon after the C.P.R. was completed in 1885, a private still was installed and operated at the foot of Cascade and Stony Squaw mountains, on the bank of the creek. It is not necessary to mention the operator's name here, suffice it to say he is now a prominent and wealthy prairie farmer. Refusing to sell a quantity of his moon-

Banff Springs Hotel staff, June 1913; *Paris Collection.*

FATAL DROWNING ACCIDENT

Crag, June 21, 1913

Montreal girls drowned in the Bow River.

Eva Vallent and Lilly Anderson of the Banff Springs Hotel staff.

While playing on a raft on the Spray river above where it empties into the Bow, Eva Vallent and Lilly Anderson were drowned. Five young men, their companions, escaped.

The party were punting the raft around in a back current of the Spray, and pushing out too far into the main current the raft swung down the Bow at 10 miles an hour. Hardly was it in the main river before it partly upset, throwing the party into the water. Mr. Bond, one of the men, pulled the girls back on the raft, the other men seizing logs and eventually got to shore. The raft then drifted as far as the golf links where it struck a pile of saw logs upsetting the raft, and the girls being sucked under the logs with a strong current were never seen again. Mr. Bond shouted to the girls to hang on to the floating logs as he was powerless to give assistance, being thrown around in the currents caused by the stranded saw logs, he eventually got to shore on a drifting log. Canoes were at once got from the boathouse, and search parties went as far as Canmore, but no sign of the girls could be found.

The Eau Clair loggers were busy along the Bow, searching for the missing girls. The men of the party were Messrs. Lennan, Shultz, Bond, Graham and Wand. All of the C.P.R. Hotel Staff.

shine product to a fellow-man, the latter turned informer with the result that the Mounted Police raided the place, destroyed the plant and worm, confiscated all the whisky that could be found and arrested the distiller. He was found guilty of moonshining and sentenced to serve a term of two years in jail.

Soon after this the Riel rebellion broke out and the prisoner was released on parole to shoulder a rifle and serve through the campaign. Returning to prison to complete the balance of his sentence, a grateful government granted the man a pardon.

The private distiller or moonshiner, call him which you will, was a wise and cautious man and had the habit of burying his surplus stock. In conversation with an intimate friend, in Calgary, very recently he volunteered the information that an oak barrel, filled to the bung-hole with the most choice brand of whisky he had ever turned out, was to the best of his knowledge and belief still reposing in its burial place along the banks of Whiskey creek.

It would appear from the above, the authenticity of which we have no just reason to doubt, that a barrel of whiskey, imprisoned for thirty years in staves of oak, awaits the successful digger along the banks of Whiskey creek. The liquid joy, no matter how it was distilled, should be almost priceless now.

That a thorough and systematic effort will be made to recover the long-buried treasure is a foregone conclusion, as conditions will be peculiarly ripe for such efforts after the first of July. In giving this secret to the world Crag and Canyon makes only one stipulation: Whoever unearths the buried treasure should, in common humanity, donate a small portion (a gallon or two) to the editor of this journal—to be used for scientific purposes.

Crag, August 25, 1919

It is rumored that a lodge of the Don'tgiveadam Society will be organized in Banff in the very near future, membership open to both sexes. The objects of the society are mutual benefit and character study, with draw poker, rummy and village scandal for diversion and recreation.

Was She a Spy?

Woman Who Posed as an Artist, is Discredited

Crag, January 2, 1915

During the latter part of last July, shortly before the arrival here of the Duke of Connaught and vice-regal party, a woman registered at the Banff Springs hotel as Mrs. Caleb Keene, F.R.P.S. Her neatly engraved cards, which she distributed freely among prominent men of the town, conveyed the information that she was a member of the London Salon and of the

Peace Day Parade, 1918; *G. and W. Fear.*

Lyceum Club, London.

One of the avowed purposes of her visit was to obtain pictures of the Duke and Duchess of Connaught with the magnificent scenery of Banff for a background. She endeavored to secure photographs of Superintendent Clarke, Dr. R.G. Brett, and H.C. McMullen and others. A sitting was arranged with Mr. and Miss McMullen to be photographed on horseback as typical westerners.

She exhibited trunks full of photographs and negatives of scenery along the C.P.R., including bridges, culverts, snowsheds, etc. She explained that she was collecting these photographs, for a photo art studio in New York, the proprietor of which was anxious to add to his already large collection.

The ci-devant Mrs. Keene, who claimed to be married to an Englishman and to have two brothers in the German army, was a brilliant conversationalist. She recited interesting tales of German fortresses, statistics of food supplies, ordinance and ammunition manufacture, etc., using technical terms to give point to her stories with which ordinary women are supposed to know little or nothing about.

A letter addressed to Mrs. Keene at the Lyceum Club, London, by Mr. McMullen, was returned to Banff on Dec 24 with the indorsation across the face of the envelope: "Not a member."

There appears but little doubt that Mrs. Keene was a link in that vast chain of spies organized and maintained by the German government, and her visit to Western Canada made solely for the purpose of gathering all information possible which might be used to advantage by the kaiser and his counsellors when the war cloud burst.

Tom Hotchkiss and Ben Short, guards at the Cave and Basin Internment Camp, circa 1916; *Dan McCowan.*

Bankhead Miner Interned

Crag, January 29, 1916

Mike Lovak, an Austrian miner at Bankhead, was examined by Supt. Clarke last week and ordered interned until the end of the war. Lovak, who has worked in the Bankhead mines for the past two or three years, filled up with hooch and boasted that he had received a communication from the Austrian consulate at Seattle offering him $1,500 to blow up the Stony creek bridge on the C.P.R. main line. Three witnesses testified to having heard him make this statement. Lovak bore an excellent reputation as a miner and a mind-his-own-business fellow until booze loosened his tongue. He has nearly $3,000 to his credit in the local bank.

Some September Morn

Crag, October 16, 1915

One afternoon last week a number of ladies, after enjoying a swim in the big pool at the Cave and Basin, adjourned to the terrace to enjoy the view. Their attention was attracted by sounds of merriment floating up from the old pool and, looking down, the ladies were shocked upon beholding some thirty live studies of "September

Film crew at play in the Cave and Basin: Peter Whyte, Lew Borzage, Lew Cody, Fern Brewster (a local girl, not an actress), Cyril Gardiner, unidentified, Bunny Dill, 1922.

Morn." Permission had been granted the aliens, preparing the ground for the construction of the new internment camp, to use the old pool and, not being provided with bathing suits, they had gone into the water au naturel, unaware of the presence of ladies. The government, to avoid all chance of a repetition, has ordered a quantity of old bathing suits to be placed at the disposal of the aliens.

LOOK THESE OVER

Crag, July 27, 1918

One of the finest collections of war souvenirs to be shown in Banff is that on exhibition at Harmon's store window and collected by Dr. Learn of Banff during his two years overseas.

The collection seems to have been the possession of one dead German. Even his skull with the holes showing where the shrapnel went through is seen in the window. His purse with the bullet hole through it, his papers, his match box, are included. Then there are his instruments of war, a large gun, several different kinds of hand grenades, the German gas mask complete, a fine German helmet, sabers and swords. The parts of three zeppelins brought down in England are very interesting. The whole collection is attractively display with Mr. Harmon's usual good taste.

LETTERS TO THE EDITOR

Banff, Alta, Jan. 5, 1914

Editor Crag and Canyon:

Dear Sir, — I should like to inquire, through the medium of your paper, why workmen of foreign nationality are preferred to men of British and Canadian birth by the officials in charge of the street improvements in Banff? A mixed gang were working on Squirrel St. on Saturday last. White men, all kinds of them, are strolling about the thoroughfares idle. The local amusements do not benefit by the foreign element, but a gang of Bohunks and Dagos may, almost at any time, be seen in the postoffice sending their money home to Southern Europe. This is supposed to be a white man's country, but the present state of affairs tends to show that a man has only to make the authorities understand that he "no savvy's" to secure employment. How long is this to go on? Surely there are enough married white men in this town to do all the work that the foreigners have been doing, whereby the money so earned would be spent in this town instead of going into the pockets of the unwashed and unwished for Slavs.

Respectfully yours,
DISGUSTED

Bankhead, Alta., Jan. 13

Editor Crag and Canyon:

Dear Sir: I see in your issue of Jan. 10 some statements and queries by one "Disgusted," and must express surprise that this individual should have allowed his disgust to so arrange the focus of his mind that he believes himself so much superior a being to the Slav and Dago, insomuch that he should be given the preference of a job "digging ditches."

But, Mr. Editor, I must confess there are quite a number of these people, as was shown by the votes tabulated in the recent elections, who sit around in times of depression like these watching for the crumbs to fall from the master's table, and snarls at his fellow worm who is able to get a few crumbs, or to be plain "a job digging a ditch."

If "Disgusted" will view the question rightly, he will find it is an economic one and not one for spite towards those patient, hard-working fellows who have left wives, children and all they hold dear in response to the glaring decoys of the emigrationn authorities, and the way most of them grapple with the adverse conditions which confront them would do credit to even "Disgusted" were he in a similar condition. They have ability, sir, and if "Disgusted" were to go through the mines at Bankhead the mine officials would point out to him, with pride, the efficient work done by these Dagos, and Slavs. And, what is more, he can call at the government office in Banff and, on inquiry, will be told of the number of

Bankhead miners, circa 1915.

Dagos and Slavs buried in the Union plot in Banff cemetery and that is the price they have paid, sir. They have a keen sense of law and order, as the records of our recent strike will show, and they can bear injustice like martyrs as shown in the Calumet, Mich., disaster a few weeks ago when some "white men" like "Disgusted" shouted a false alarm of "fire" into crowded Italian hall of the strikers, where women and children had gathered to receive Christmas cheer, resulting in the death of about 80 of them. And that they have a profound feeling of independence was shown by the way they refused all outside aid in their hour of affliction.

"This is supposed to be a white man's country..."

All this and much more will continue so long as men like "Disgusted" cannot use their brains to better advantage than to fall out with what he terms Bohunks and Dagos over the "digging of a ditch." To me, Mr. Editor, it is a sign of the times and, I feel, the beginning of the end. Thanking you for the use of your columns to reply on behalf of these people I am

Yours very respectfuly.
FRANK WHEATLEY,
Sec. Miners Union
Bankhead, Alta.

Crag, September 9, 1916

One evening last week a "colored gentleman" visitor, with that spirit of southern chivalry for which so many coons are decorated by Judge Lynch, followed a couple of ladies who were walking on the streets of Banff. He did not accost them but kept close to their heels for several blocks. Passing the business place of the husband of one of the ladies, the situation was explained and the husband, slipping out the back door and executing a flank movement, took a hand in the tag game. A few minutes sufficed to prove the coon was "it" and he received a lesson he will not soon forget. The negro was a husky brute but he was as a child in the hands of the indignant husband, who tatooed the countenance of the black beast until his father, the devil, wouldn't recognize him.

Jim Sing, circa 1916.

MAYBESO TONG WAR IN BANFF

Crag, September 27, 1919

Fire broke out in the kitchen of the Silver Grill restaurant at an early hour last Saturday morning, doing considerable damage to the interior of the building, the fixtures and the Chinese proprietor's stock in trade.

The blaze was evidently of incendiary origin, a five gallon can which had contained coal oil being found behind the door leading into the restaurant from the kitchen.

No suspicion attaches to the proprietor of the Grill, who had no insurance upon his stock.

It is currently rumored that the Chinese population of Banff is divided into factions, between which bitter rivalry exists. Many citizens incline to the belief that some tool of one of these factions is responsible for the fire. In which event, it might be an act of wisdom to round up the entire bunch of Chinks and run all suspects out of the park before they burn down the village in their efforts to "get even" with one another.

Give Them a Sqaure Deal

Crag, July 10, 1920

A Chinaman is looked upon by the great majority of people in something of the light of an ox or an ass—to be beaten and kicked whenever the inclination arises and is supposed to have no come-back. We hold no belief for the Celestials, but contend that when a Chinaman pays his head tax for admission into this country he is entitled to the same justice and consideration extended to any other man of foreign extraction.

The Chinese perform duties at which "white" men turn up their noses in disdain, yet these duties are necessary and someone must do them. When left alone the Chinese are never quarrelsome, they never appear in the police court for being drunk on the streets or in public places and raising "Cain" generally, and they seldom if ever interfere with their "white" neighbors.

'Tis true they smoke opium and gamble. But men of other nationalities smoke tobacco and play poker. Where is the difference? Why not give them at least a square British deal?

Kananaskis? Sometimes

Crag, July 5, 1919

They were motoring up from the city to spend the weekend in the mountains. She was a winsome, soulful lassie of some nineteen sun-kissed summers and hot-house winters, with heart-strings keyed in responsive echo to the June song nature was singing, while her eyes photographed on the book of memory the scenic grandeur along the trail. He was a callow youth with brain capable of but one idea, and that was centered upon the newly-acquired car he was driving.

Yearning for a little loving sympathy with her keen enjoyment of the journey she sought for some means of awakening the youth at her side to a sense of the vanishing opportunities, when the sign Kananaskis caught her attention.

"Kan-an-as-kis?" she gurgled interrogatively (lingering over the syllables), and pressing her shoulder against his, "Do you really think so?"

"Oh, yes," said the young man, giving the wheel a wrench to avoid a rock in the road.

Waiting patiently and expectantly for half an hour, while the engine sang the song of the road, the maiden broke the silence with "I believe that sign is a wicked lie," and gazed meditatively, with tear-dimmed eyes, at the distant hills all gowned in the twilight haze.

A Banff Idyll

Fate Threw Cold Water on Love's Young Dream

Crag, July 14, 1914

Synopsis: A pretty girl, a gay young man, a perfect June day in Banff the beautiful, a gaily painted canoe, a sparkling stream—and an accession to the ranks of the Baptists by involuntary immersion.

She was a sweet young thing with a longing for a few hours surcease from the heat, dust and turmoil of life in the oil city. She came to Banff the beautiful last Sunday morning to gratify her longings amidst the natural beauties and romantic surroundings of this earthly paradise for young twain whose hearts beat as one—sometimes. She arrived clothed in smiles, anticipations of joy unconfined and other articles of apparel convention renders necessary, in the shape of frills, fluffy lingerie, furbelows and flounces.

He is a resident of Banff, with a heart big enough to embrace all girldom had it not been filled with the image of "the one girl" from the oil city. He met the train and the girl, escorted her to the zoo and pointed with pride to the cage where the wolverine was—but is not now—showered peanuts on the girl, himself and the monkeys and spent the morning hours in blissful unconsciousness of what an unkind fate had in store for him.

After dinner a canoe was procured, the happy couple embarked and paddled up Forty-mile creek. Lost to a sense of all danger, drinking intoxicating draughts of happiness from the bright eyes and smiling lips of the girls, while the matchless scenery glided unheeded past, fate dealt the gay Lothario a cold deck. A false motion of the paddle, a sudden swerving of the fragile craft, a scream, a prayer word—and the man and the girl were struggling in the embrace of the cold waters.

Lorne and Anna May Orr, circa 1905; *Whyte Collection.*

What might have resulted in tragedy was fortunately averted by the timely arrival of another boat upon the scene, the couple were fished out of the water and landed safely. But alas, for the frills and fluffy lingerie—their

Paris Tearoom waitresses, circa 1924; *Fulton Dunsmore.*

bright, bewitching, man-catching glory had departed.

Crag, October 21, 1916

It cost the manager at one of the Banff hotels, recently closed, $7.50 for a kiss—which he didn't get—from one of his chambermaids. The manager was graciously bidding the employees farewell, when he allowed his eye to linger with desire upon the charms of a comely chambermaid and he endeavored to impress an osculatory embrace upon her ripe, red, pouting lips. The maid was not willing and, in the struggle which followed, a lens in the manager's eyeglasses was broken. The cost of a new lens was $7.50—the record price in Banff for a kiss which wasn't a kiss.

Crag, July 15, 1922

The next time a certain young lady tells Harry to "leave her alone" he will pay heed, especially if the dog is anywhere in the vicinity. The dog loves his mistress, his teeth are very sharp and it costs money to repair rents in trousers.

Crag, September 13, 1919

These cold nights turn thoughts of lonely bachelors to the problem of getting married or buying a coal oil heater.

Crag, July 5, 1919

Riding horseback a pillion may have looked picturesque in ye olden days, but it is inhumanity to both biped and quadruped for two people of the opposite sex to parade the streets these days perched on the quarter deck of a long-suffering cayuse, looks vulgar and is detrimental to dignity and—panties.

Cave and Basin, 1916; *C.B. Brown.*

Cave and Basin, circa 1920; *Whyte Collection.*

Crag, August 2, 1919

A Thing resembling a man has been amusing himself at the Cave and Basin swimming pool by grabbing women bathers and ducking them. It mattered not that the women were strangers to the silly ass and objected to his handling—he goes right ahead with the Cave Man stuff. A sound thrashing and an order to move out of the park should be handed the bounder right speedily, or Banff will become a by-word as a place to avoid by decent tourists.

"Lady of the Lake," 1908; F.W. Freeborn.

Local News Notes

Crag, July 2, 1921

Walter Ashdown, a jitney driver, in an endeavor to demonstrate to a companion the blow that would settle the world's championship fight, sustained a fractured wrist.

Crag, July 30, 1921

Bob Edwards paid his first visit to the Cave last Sunday, it having taken him 25 years to find it. He remarked in a soulful manner, "It's strange such a wet place should be so dry."

Crag, September 9, 1916

A man would be given a joy-ride in a patrol wagon if he ventured on the street clad in a suit made from striped awning: but a woman can get away with it.

Crag, May 14, 1920

A Canmore Lothario eloped with a married woman of Banff this week. When the awakening comes they will both probably decide they have made a bad bargain.

No Lady at All

Crag, September 29, 1917

The lady who lost a diamond ring in the Basin a week ago last Saturday as reported in Crag and Canyon, was no lady at all, so Mr. Walker informs us. She was a gentleman. But then some gentlemen have long hair, and some ladies have moustaches, so that it is pretty hard to tell which is which with bathing suits on.

Messrs. Barnett and Spencer, circa 1916. On the occasion of a royal visit, Mr. Barnett, the street sweeper, was the only person in Banff capable of writing a properly worded address; *Dan McCowan.*

Frank Beattie, circa 1916; *Dan McCowan.*

Crag, July 31, 1925

Mr. John Barnett will be seventy-six in January of next year; he was born on Lord Rothchild's estate, at Alton, Buckinghamshire, England.

Mr. Barnett, fondly called "Dad" by many of the townspeople can be seen daily at his work keeping the streets of Banff clean and tidy and when he comes along with his brush all have to move before him, including cars and everything. Nobody gives him orders, he is his own boss—monarch of all he surveys on the streets of Banff.

Crag, September 13, 1919

One young lady, whose birthday anniversary occurs on the 17th, is wondering whether the Prince of Wales had been informed of that fact and timed his visit here accordingly.

James "Nigger Bill" Davie, circa 1916. Bill later owned the White Help Café which had a Chinese cook.
Dan McCowan.

George "Ockey" Fowles, 1916. The Crag reported he sold the magazines at the prices printed on the covers.
Dan McCowan.

Crag, July 15, 1916

A bit of excitement was caused last Saturday night by the announcement that the little daughter of Byron Harmon was lost. A number of volunteers turned out and after an hour's search the little tot was found fast asleep in her father's theatre.

Banff Advocate, September 12, 1919

Stefansson, the Arctic explorer, returned to his camp at Spray Lake this week, where in the solitude of the mountains he is writing the story of his experiences in the frozen north.

Crag, July 30, 1921

Professor Fay, of Tuft's University, Boston, is here to attend the Alpine camp at Lake O'Hara. The professor, although 75 years old, is still an enthusiastic mountaineer and rarely if ever misses the annual gathering of the club.

Indian Days, Banff Avenue, circa 1920; *Whyte Collection.*

Crag, August 8, 1914

Carl Rungius, the noted artist who sketches with his left hand and paints with his right, expects to arrive here early next month for his annual painting trip among the mountains. Mr. Rungius is at present in Germany but is scheduled to arrive in New York on the 27th inst. Many of his paintings and sketches decorate Banff homes and are highly prized by their fortunate possessors.

Crag, July 5, 1919

Prof. Walcott, of the Smithsonian Institute, Washington, D.C. with Mrs. Walcott have arrived for their summer's work in the Rockies.

"WINDS OF CHANCE"

Filmed at Banff

Crag, December 4, 1925

If sacrifices are essential to achievement, Frank Lloyd's "Winds of Chance," which is to show at the Lux Theatre next Monday and Tuesday, December 7th and 8th, can boast of mishaps which interrupted production.

On a first trip to location the company, aboard a Canadian Pacific train, was wrecked by a rockslide near Thompson Lake, Alberta, and miraculously escaped disaster. The engine was completely knocked off the track and demolished, killing the engineer. The Lloyd players were one car behind the

Filming Valley of the Silent Men, 1922, on Tunnel Mountain; Frank Borzage and Alma Rubens as hero and heroine.

three that followed the engine from the track and were battered by falling rocks.

Three days later, at Lake Minnewanka, a snowslide tossed cameras and several players off an icy ledge of a glacier.

Viola Dana passed through an earthquake en route to meet the company. Tom London dislocated three vertebrae in a fall. Victor McLaglen came near drowning in the rapids. A carpenter broke his leg under a heavy barge at the edge of the rapid.

Lloyd was twice thrown into the rapids by rough water. Vaccination at the border caused several players to be too ill to appear before the camera for a week, and a warm sun melted a perfectly good three-foot snow fall which covered the Dawson City set and threatened to ruin one of the biggest scenes of the picture.

But after all of the unforseen trouble which hampered progress the gods were kind and "Winds of Chance" was finished with unusual enthusiasm and realism.

CROWD ENJOYS SUNDAY BAND CONCERT

Crag, August 28, 1925

The Banff Citizens' Band, under the very capable leadership of Fred A. Bagley, are presenting to the citizens of Banff and visitors, some very find band concerts on Sunday evenings. Those who wish to attend church service on Sunday evenings have ample time to get to the Lux Theatre where the concerts are held.

Mr. and Mrs. Vernon first of all gave a saxophone duet, accompanied by Mr. and Mrs. Wm. Selwyn on violin and piano. This number demanded a great deal of applause and was followed by a trombone novelty number. Mr. Vernon supplied the "wind" for the notes necessary while Mrs. Vernon operated the trombone slide. This made a great hit with the audience. It was undoubtedly a very clever accomplishment and deserved all the applause tendered.

The Vernons, 1925; *Byron Harmon.*

$62,000 BLAZE

Destroying King Edward Hotel Block Saturday Morning

Criminal Negligence by Government Officials

Crag, February 14, 1914

One of the most spectacular and destructive fires in the history of Banff occurred last Saturday morning, resulting in the destruction of the frame portion of the King Edward hotel block. The building was three stories, 66 x 86, and contained the J.D. Anderson tailoring establishment, the O K Electric shop, the King Edward Bar and the Lux theatre, all fronting on Banff avenue. At the rear was the hotel office, sample rooms and lavatories. The upper stories contained 50 bedrooms, unoccupied in winter except by hotel employees.

The fire was first discovered at 9 o'clock in a room over the O K Electric shop. The alarm was given and the hotel employees got busy with the hotel hose. But it was soon evident that out-

Fire at the King Edward Hotel, 1911.

side help was needed to cope with the blaze, owing to difficulty in locating it, and a general alarm was sent out.

The clang of the fire bell brought the volunteer fire brigade and hundreds of citizens speedily on the scene and the fire hose was quickly connected with the nearest hydrant, only to discover the hydrant was frozen solid and the united efforts of a dozen men failed to move it. Other near-by hydrants were tried and found in like useless condition.

"...the hydrant was frozen solid and the united efforts of a dozen men failed to move it."

The chemical engine was brought to the fire but was found to be useless as the man paid by the government to look after it had neglected to keep the engine charged with the necessary chemicals. By the time this negligence was rectified the fire had gained too great headway for the chemical to be of any avail.

In the meantime, after a half hour's waste of precious time, water was obtained from Cariboo and Bear street hydrants but many sections of hose, which had been thoughtfully stored

Peter Whyte at the wheel, George MacLean (Chief Walking Buffalo) in the bison horn headdress, Jonas Benjamin in the middle, and Dan Wildman with the rifle, and two other Stoney Indians; the car is a 1923 Hudson; Bow Avenue, Banff; *Whyte Collection.*

Banff Indian Days parade, circa 1916.

Banff Indian Days, circa 1925; *Byron Harmon.*

out-of-doors all winter at the mercy of the elements, were unfit for service, the couplings freezing solid as soon as cold water touched them.

Meanwhile the bales of hay, fervent cuss words and other inflammable material had been piled around the frozen hydrants, lighted and, after an hour's delay, water was available. The blaze, however, had not even waited for telegraphic permission from Ottawa and the frame part of the hotel was a mass of seething flame.

Charlie Beil with ice sculpture. Charlie, a well-known sculptor in bronze, carved the bison for the 1938 Winter Carnival. The local bank manager, passing by while Charlie was at work, complimented him on his work. Charlie inquired if he could use it as collateral for a loan. The banker replied he couldn't grant loans on frozen assets; *Byron Harmon.*

The efforts of the firefighters were then confined to an endeavor to save the brick hotel and the Brewster Trading Co's store. For a time it looked as though their efforts would be futile, but a gamer bunch of men never manned a fire hose and they stayed on the job until the Brewster building was safe and the brick addition to the hotel, 36 x 130 feet, although badly scorched and gutted, was wrested from the clutches of the fire fiend.

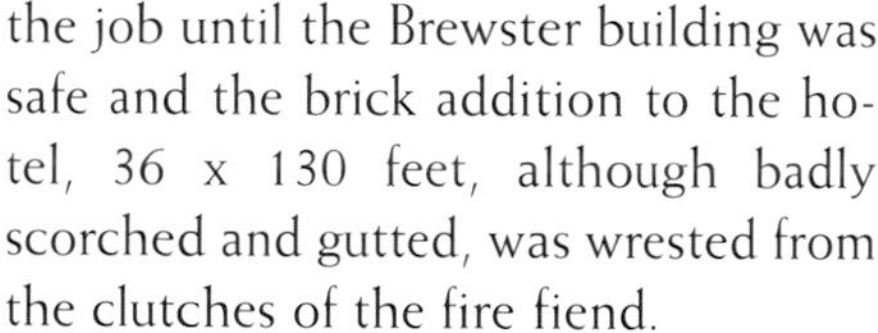

The building burned very slowly owing to the heavy material used in its construction. Had the hydrants been in working order, the fire could easily have been confined to the rooms where it originated.

Crag, February 14, 1925

This is where the first spirit of co-operation always shown by local businessmen and citizens comes to the fore. In past years the committee has learned some hard, costly lessons, but through experience they have been taught that a grocery store has a grocer in charge, a hardware store a hardware man and in a village of beavers a beaver rules, and in this carnival it was necessary to apply business methods and let businessmen rule. The result amply demonstrates that this variety of prudent judgement will be hereafter more widely demanded.

At present the town is in the state of reaching feverishly for pre-eminence as a winter resort. There is an active local pride constantly striving for "something big" for the town. The fever has reached all and sundry and in time will reach places where real help will be given, especially if the fever is properly incubated by local boosters, who de-

Winter Carnival, Banff Avenue, 1929; *Byron Harmon.*

sire the town to progress and grow as a real winter resort.

Sometimes under stress like this well-meaning boosters often lead young organizations into improvident debt.

The winter sports association is composed mainly of men who are mindful of this, having seen the town grow to be a summer resort without peer in the world, and by exercising the proper amount of caution have safely escorted the 1925 winter carnival over the shoals without financial loss and made many of the old ideas do until the need of new ones is inescapable, believing that it is good business to pay for the old coat before cutting cloth for the new one.

About the carnival itself, it would be hard to deal with it in detail. It was a big affair and drew well. Banff's scenic charm and wonderful show places in the park are enough to draw visitors. But those who came to the carnival are certain that what has made the town a popular summer playground can be repeated in winter if the same attractive features are offered again.

Locally Banff has developed a zest for winter sports of the kind that the individual participates in, and especially amongst the younger people. If necessary the younger people could stage an attractive program at short notice that would please a most critical audience. This is the result of fostering and promoting our national pastimes under proper guidance and organization. Visitors were struck with the idea that no

Snowmobile, circa 1925.

"Dog pitch," Winter Carnival, circa 1925; *Byron Harmon.*

Snowshoe obstacle race, circa 1925; *George Noble.*

child in town walked in the customary manner, the boy or girl either trudged along on skis, travelled on snowshoes, mushed behind a dog sleigh or toboggan. This gave visitors the right impetus and spirit to get into the game too, and in this way solved one of the committee's most perplexing problems, that of entertaining visitors between acts.

Crag, January 3, 1915

To W.H. Kidner, more than any other member of the Banff Winter Sports club, is due the credit for having a slide this winter.

"Swish," Erling Strom skiing near Elizabeth Lake, Mount Assiniboine, circa 1935; *Nicholas Morant.*

And now, there remains but one thing more to make the slide the success it should be, and that is some general order or rule by the Winter Sports club regarding the position to be assumed on the toboggan. An effort was made last winter to compel people using the slide to lie down on the toboggan, and many people still imagine that rule is in force. Such a position is not only ungraceful but vulgar, and tends to keep many ladies from enjoying the delights of tobagganing. To lie down on one's stomach and have one or more lie on top of one might "go" with children of tender years, but to the average woman such a posture is not only undignified, but savors too much of the "tango," "turkey trot," etc., to appeal to them.

No such rule exists on the books of the club, and people using the slide may exercise their own inclination as to the manner of occupying the toboggan. But it is not only safer and saner to sit on the toboggan, but more graceful and dignified, and we opine that scores of ladies who have remained away on account of the mistaken idea that they must lie down on the toboggan, would show their appreciation of a rule to the effect that sitting up was "the thing" by thronging the slide and enjoying to the full the delights of that king of winter sports.

Russell Bennett at work locating the girl in the avalanche, 1929; *Erlig Strom.*

Quest for Ore, Russell Bennett, 1963

With a party of friends I was skiing, in the winter of 1929, the slopes around Mount Assiniboine, in the Canadian Rockies. Our party was crossing, strung out single file, a slope high up on Goat Mountain. Three had gone across and were safely on the other side. A girl was ahead of me, who was last in the file. Suddenly I felt a shock beneath my skis and hear the ominous crr-ump. I looked up and saw the breaking surf under the cliffs. I pushed off down slope, turned through the fall line, and headed for the rocky comb that bounded the snow field. I just made it; the instant before my skis scraped the rock I felt the surface beneath them weaving.

I turned and looked back. Where there had been before a satiny white slope there was now only a tumbled mass of snow blocks, and the figure of the girl had vanished. I flung out upon the broken surface, which was so rough I fell every second step. I became aware of the shouts of my companions across the slope, and saw them pointing down below me. I stumbled in that direction, saw nothing, pulled up, and saw them pointing and shouting again. At last I caught it; there was a small black object above the broken surface. I reached it, and found it to be the upper portion of a black ski mitten. I dug frantically, soon joined by two of my companions, both veterans of the snow slopes. They were Erling Strom and the Marquis of Albizzi. We followed the arm down, and there, unharmed but curled up in a tight ball, with skis pointing backwards over her shoulders, was the girl. She had not been long enough in the trap to exhaust the available air, but she was as firmly held in the snow as though she had been encased in concrete. When an avalanche comes to rest its snow, however powdery when flowing, freezes, under the phenomenon of regelation, into a hard mass.

Mrs. Stone Tells World for First Time Details of Mount Eon Tragedy

Calgary Herald, July 29, 1921

Herald Staff Correspondent Secures Interview As She Lies In an Improvised Fly Camp Pitched Near the Scene Of the Fatality—Had Almost Reached Summit Of Virgin Peak When Husband Either Stepped on Loose Rock or Lost His Handhold and Fell Past Her Into Deep Chasm

MRS. STONE MAKES VALIANT ATTEMPT TO GO TO RESCUE

Grips on Rope Fails and She Drops, but Descent Is Broken By Narrow Ledge, Where for Eight Days, Without Food or Water, Bruised and Broken, She Waits Patiently for the End to Come—Swiss Guide Finds Her Unconscious and Performs Remarkable Feat in Removing Her to Safety

MARVEL CREEK, JULY 29,

(by pony express and telegraph)

Suffering from starvation and shock, Mrs. Stone is lying in an improvised fly camp on the side of Mount Eon, while the party who rescued her are busy building a raft to convey her down the Marvel lakes, the first stage of the 55-mile trip to civilization. The search for Dr. Stone her husband, has proved unavailing so far and the rescue party are nearly exhausted from their efforts to find him. It is probable that the body, for Dr. Stone is dead, will be left until another and better equipped search party can be organized.

TRAPPED ON SIDE OF PRECIPICE

After having been trapped on the side of a precipice for eight days, without food or water, terribly bruised and realizing that her husband must be dead somewhere beneath her, Mrs. Stone is in wonderful condition. True, she is weak, but Dr. Bell, of Winnipeg, who was one of the rescue party and who has been with her since she was found on Sunday, is confident that she is now out of danger. Though she has had little more than an hour's sleep since she was found, and little nourishment, on Wednesday evening she was able to speak briefly of her terrible experience. During the greater part of the time, however, the rescue party have been unable to converse with her except at odd intervals.

HOW DR. STONE FELL

The accident in which Dr. Stone lost his life occurred on Saturday, July 16, and not on Sunday as was at first believed. Mrs. Stone has been able to relate some of the circumstances. On Friday she and her husband set out to climb the south-eastern slope of Mount Eon, near Mount Assiniboine.

Opposite: A.H. McCarthy, Dr. W.E. Stone, C.F. Hodgboom, Dr. W.A. Liincoln, on Naiset Peak, ACC Annual Camp, Mount Assiniboine, 1920; *Harry Pollard.*

They established a fly camp on the slope of the mountain, and on Saturday morning commenced the ascent. They climbed without being fastened together by a rope. In the afternoon they had nearly reached the summit and were negotiating a particularly stiff bit of almost perpendicular cliff. Mr. Stone was slightly in advance. As Mrs. Stone looked up toward her husband she believes that he stepped on a loose rock or else a handhold on the mountain side broke away. Instantly he fell, and as he went past Mrs. Stone she saw him strike the face of the cliff several times, his body turning over and over until in a twinkling he disappeared into the grim abyss below.

"...her fall was broken about 10 feet from the end of the rope by a tiny ledge"

MRS. STONE'S GAME ATTEMPT

Without stopping to count the cost and without realizing the impossibility of saving her husband's life, Mrs. Stone prepared to go to the rescue. Fastening a rope which she carried to the mountain side, she climbed rapidly down. When she reached the end of the rope, she found no foot or hand hold, and dangled against the cliff, 1,000 feet from the ground. For some time she hung there, then being unable to make her way up the rope again and finding nothing else to cling to, she relaxed her hold on her slender life line. Fate intervened to save Mrs. Stone from instant death, for below her the cliff sheered away abruptly for a thousand feet before a more gradual slope could be found. Dropping, her fall was broken about 10 feet from the end of the rope by a tiny ledge, not four feet wide. Here, without food or water, with little to hold to, she remained for eight long days.

CLINGS TO LONE CHANCE

During that time clouds often surrounded the mountain top and frequent storms accompanied by vivid lightning and thunder broke about her. Long ere help arrived she must have despaired of ever being rescued but her wonderful stamina carried her through, and caused her to cling to the faint chance for life. On Friday night, by a forced march, Rudolph Aemmer, Billy Childs, Bill Peyto and the mounted policeman, Pounders, arrived at Mount Eon. Previous to this, members of the government trail gang at Marvel Creek, knowing that the Stones were lost, had searched for them, but unsuccessfully.

GUIDE'S REMARKABLE FEAT

It was just after supper on Sunday evening that Aemmer, the Swiss guide, found Mrs. Stone. Letting himself down to her ledge with a rope, he fastened the rope about her body, a difficult task, for she was terribly bruised. Drawing her up to where a foothold could be gained, he performed what Gen. Mitchell describes as a wonderful

Fred Ballard on Mount Edith, circa 1900; *Paris Collection.*

feat, for he carried the unconscious woman down the face of the mountain in his arms.

At the present time an arduous journey remains for Mrs. Stone, for the trail to Banff is 55 miles of pack horse trail, beset with many difficulties. She must be carried on a stretcher every foot of the way, with the exception of the short span of the Marvel lakes.

STORMS ARE FREQUENT

Thunder storms with heavy rains, which have been very numerous during the past two days, are not conducive to easy travel, especially when an invalid must be taken care of, and this further complicates matters. The work of the rescue party scouring Mount Eon from Friday to Thursday has been terribly hard and the members of the little band are not far from exhausted themselves.

Banff Avenue, circa 1917.

REFLECTIONS

Crag, September 8, 1917

For the tourist who visited Banff, say twenty years ago, the Banff of today would seem a different spot—a different world. Then to the resident every tourist was known, even to his habits, his peculiarities, his place of abode and his family history.

> *"Then Banff had not become commercialized. Today it has."*

Now the average tourist passes through our gates and no one knows of his comings or goings, and he may be here today and gone tomorrow without arousing any local interest whatever. The reason is not far to seek. The tourist travel to Banff has developed and increased to such an extent that the town, during the summer months, is about as cosmopolitan in its population as any town of its size of the North American continent. Then again with the increase in population in the Province the travel to Banff has increased accordingly.

To those of us who were here in the early days and who know Banff in its natural restfulness, the change which has come about, seems almost a sacrilege. Where today the automobile purrs and honks and rushes the traveller hither and thither, then the tourist was content to jog along behind a team of horses or to ride the reluctant cayuse and take time enough to admire and absorb the reve-

Mollie Adams, Mary T.S. Schäffer, Billy Warren, 1907. After the death of Mrs. Schäffer's husband she and Miss Adams, a geology professor at Columbia University, took extensive packtrips in the Rockies, reaching Maligne Lake from Laggan in 1908; *Mary I.S. Schäffer.*

lation of the Divine, in mountain, in stream and in canyon.

Then Banff had not become commercialized. Today it has. We know that modern civilization demands certain improvements and sanitary conveniences, and we know that the government has endeavored to assist nature and to improve conditions, generally. In some ways they have brought about improvements, in others they have undone God's work and given little in return.

The Banff of twenty years ago was a restful spot. You did not have to wait a chance to jump into the basin. The roads were cut out of the virgin trees and shrubbery. There seemed to be many paths and trails where Nature had not been disturbed and where Silence lent a charm to Beauty. Where the hand of man had not defaced the handiwork of the Creator and where the eternal peaks were in keeping with the intervening valleys. The Banff of today is largely a modern creation. We have the dust which follows the track of the multitude; the cement sidewalks; the cleared-out shrubbery; the zoo with its victims of thraldom; turnstiles at the Cave and Basin and the Hot Springs and many other innovations.

Mary T.S. Schäffer, letters to Raymond Zillmer

Stoney Indians, circa 1920; *Byron Harmon.*

January 2, 1928

I am wondering who took over that wonderful trail, for after all, it all depends on the man in the lead and his horses. We have about four good guides here in Banff.

Lewis Freeman is most incorrect for one who has gone over that country so many times. Jim Simpson and I have had many a laugh after we got over our indignation when he wrote and got into the National Geographic that awful article. Harmon's pictures were wonderful. It was a waste of honest cash for me to buy Freeman's book because he simply was either a mighty poor trailer or a very imaginative one. I have been lying in wait for him to ask him a few questions. Think of the times I have gone round Bow Lake, the simplest lake imaginable. Have you tried it? I am sure you must and he just had to imagine all its terrors to get off such rot. Often I think how useless it is to write or rather read real travel. For the fellow who knows about it is apt to stick up his nose. I have lived among the explorers of other than our dear mountains and really they do tell fibs.

February 28, 1928

Let's shake hands on Freeman. I know Harmon very well and for the life of me, I could not see why he did not want either Jimmie Simpson or myself (the only people who knew the nature of the route at the time) to meet the man. The moment the book was issued, I knew. It was disgusting to me and I wanted to write Gilbert Grosvenor and tell him I could never believe in his old Geographic magazine again. By the way, you should meet old Jim. We have many fine guides here, but Jim is the last of the old regime. He fails to look like anything but himself, which is not

"We have many fine guides here, but Jim is the last of the old regime."

Bow Lake, 1924; *Byron Harmon.*

much, a grin that nothing wipes off, educated, an artist and a beautiful shot. His house is a very interesting one as he escorted all the best people who have come to Banff into the hills for a number of years. The artists ALWAYS get him, and his home is a treasure trove of their work, Carl Rungius, Belmore Brown, Fuertes, etc. He is musical, and he knows how to make every horse take his place in line and keep it. After Jim saw that thing of Freeman's, he wrote to the Geographic and said not to waste any more stamps sending him such rot. Yes, we have been all over that part of the way. I don't LOOK like a goat but I think I have acted like one for in all the valleys through which we passed, it seems to me I have taken a flit.

STAFF AT PLAY

Crag, June 15, 1918

When Manager Benaglia selected his staff for the Banff Springs hotel there isn't the slightest doubt about it but that his aesthetic eye took in form, figure, features and accomplishments of those who should be permitted to bask in summer sunshine for the season in Banff. The evidence was available in bunches at the Staff dance given in the hotel ball room on Monday night last. On the female side of the staff there were blondes, brunettes and intermediates—all as pretty as pictures—and with features which when framed in a Gainsborough or any other kind of a lid, would be so alluring that no mere man could look them

Madeleine Pedlar, the singer with Horace Lapp's Orchestra, being serenaded at the Banff Springs Hotel. Circa 1935; *Nicholas Morant.*

straight in the eye and deny them anything their little hearts desired, and the best of it is that the prettiest of them are the most accomplished and talented. On the male side form and sprightliness predominated, but then nobody is interested in the men these days.

As befitted the auspices under which the festivities were scheduled, the dance commenced right on the dot when Manager Benaglia slipped from the crowd, slid to the well-prepared floor, and with his partner amidst an admiring crowd eliminated the whale dip, the shark flop and other fancy capers.

Crag, August 6, 1921

An American tourist of the female persuasion took in the sights at Sundance Canyon last week. After exhausting her vocabulary over the scenery she remarked to a companion: "These mountains are growing older and beginning to show their age. They look considerably dirtier than when I was here seven years ago."

Crag, July 23, 1921

Two ladies, tourists, were in the Mount Royal rotunda one night recently when a member of the local

A still for Cameron of the Mounted, a Hollywood production filmed at Bankhead, near Banff. Corporal Taylor, Banff detachment, RCMP, is the authentic Mountie, the one not kissing his horse. Circa 1920.

detachment of the R.C.M.P. entered the telegraph office adjacent. One of the ladies nudged her companion and in an audible whisper said: "Look at that, the hall porters are dressed in such unusual uniforms. But why does he tote a gun?" The mountie had his side arms on.

Crag, June 10, 1922

Jiggs" the Johnson Canyon bear, has added a new accomplishment to his list—a desire to hug women. Which only goes to prove that the dividing line between men and animals—some of both, at least—is purely imaginary.

Crag, September 13, 1919

More parties are going out on the trail from Banff this season than ever before in the history of the village, and it is taxing the outfitting companies to supply the demand for guides, horses, etc.

The Banff Springs hotel will close for the season on the 30th inst., and the cliff-dwellers will perforce be compelled to come down to ordinary hotel

Stills taken during the filing of "A Game of Golf" on the Banff Springs Hotel course.

life and fare—which is better than they get at the big wigwam, even if it cost two-thirds less.

While there is no longer a crowd of people on the streets day and night, Banff is by no means a deserted village. The hotels are well filled and cottagers are still coming to enjoy a holiday in the mountains, which are beginning to don their autumn robes.

The Sanitarium hotel closed after breakfast Monday morning. Manager Scarth has had one of the most successful seasons in his management of the San., and does not believe in losing any of the garnered shekels by keeping the hotel open after the cream is skimmed off the tourist business.

Tommy Tweed, then a Brewster driver, later a distinguished actor and playwright, is in the armour playing Jacob Twoyoungman, a Stoney chief, while Mary Douglas, a hotel employee, caddies. Circa 1935; *Nicholas Morant.*

Text Sources and Bibliography

The greatest number of texts have been extracted from the *Crag and Canyon*, a weekly newspaper published in Banff since 1900, cited as *Crag* and followed by the date of publication.

Several longer texts have been drawn from the *Canadian Alpine Journal (CAJ)*, the annual journal of the Alpine Club of Canada, the *American Alpine Journal (AAJ)*, the annual of the American Alpine Club, and *Appalachia*, the publication of the Appalachian Mountain Club.

The balance of the textual material comes from printed sources published in books, and some hitherto unpublished archival material in the Archives of the Canadian Rockies.

Bennett, Russell H., *Quest for Ore*, Minneapolis: T.S. Dennison & Company, Inc., 1963.

Campbell, Robert E., *I Would Do It Again*, Toronto: The Ryerson Press, 1959.

Griesbach, W.A., *I Remember*, Toronto: The Ryerson Press, 1946.

Interior Reports, 1886, Department of the Interior, Government of Canada.

Lees, J.A., and W.J. Clutterbuck, B.C.1887, *A Ramble in British Columbia*, London: Longmans, Green & Co., 1892.

Liddell, Ken, *I'll Take the Train*, Saskatoon: Modern Press, Prairie Books, 1966.

Mitchell, B.W. *Trail Life in the Canadian Rockies*, New York: The Macmillan Company, 1924.

Roberts, Morley, *The Western Avernus*, London: Archibald Constable, 1896.

Shaw, Charles Aeneas, *Tales of a Pioneer Surveyor*, Don Mills: Longman Canada, 1970.

Sladen, Douglas, *On the Cars and Off*, London: Ward, Lock, and Bowden, Limited, 1895.

Stutfield, Hugh E.M., and J. Norman Collie, *Climbs and Explorations in the Canadian Rockies*, London: Longmans, Green & Co., 1903.

Wilcox, Walter D., *The Rockies of Canada*, New York and London: G.P. Putman's Sons, 1909.

AUTHOR NOTES

The following text extracts are copyright by other owners, and we have endeavoured to seek permission to include them in Rocky Mountain Madness.

Shaw, Charles Aeneas, *Tales of a Pioneer Surveyor,* edited by Raymond Hull, © 1970; Liddell, Ken, *"I'll Take the Train",* © 1966; Griesbach, W.A., *I Remember,* © 1946; Bennett, Russell H., *Quest for One,* © 1963; Mitchell, B.W., *Trail Life in the Canadian Rockies,* © 1924; Campbell, Robert E., *I would do it Again,* © 1959; Roberts, Morley, *On the Old Trail,* © 1927

The photographs and other visual materials in Rocky Mountain Madness are principally copyrighted by the Archives of the Canadian Rockies, the Peter and Catharine Whyte Foundation, Banff, Alberta, Canada, which also houses the photographic collections of the Alpine Club of Canada. Other institutions whose works are used with permission are herein noted: Canadian Pacific Corporate Archives: pp. 128, 138, 140, and 141; Glenbow Alberta Institute: pp. 47, and 126; City of Vancouver Archives: pg. 16; Provincial Archives of Alberta: pp. 19, 23 top, 38 bottom, 46, and 73.

Edward Cavell selected the photographs while Curator of Photography at the Whyte Museum of the Canadian Rockies in Banff. He is the author of *Journeys to the Far West, A Delicate Wilderness, Legacy in Ice* and *Sometimes a Great Nation.* For *Rocky Mountain Madness* he reviewed more than a hundred thousand photographs.

Jon Whyte (1941-1992) edited the texts while Curator of Banff Heritage Homes, Whyte Museum of the Canadian Rockies. Poet, columnist, writer and film maker, he is the author of *Gallimaufry, Homage, Henry Kelsey,* and contributed to many anthologies, magazines, and other outlets. His best guess was that he read more than 2,000,000 words in seeking out the texts for *Rocky Mountain Madness.*

Colonel Ffrench-O'Brien greeting a bear. He later became a friend of Ian Fleming and served as the model for the character of James Bond.